Saints of the
New Testament

Saints of the New Testament

Written by
Rev. Victor Hoagland, C. P.

Edited by
Evelyn Bence

Regina Press
New York

THE REGINA PRESS
10 Hub Drive
Melville, New York

ISBN 0-88271-646-8

Printed in Belgium.

Table of Contents

Introduction

Mary, Joseph, Peter, John, Martha and Mary...familiar names from the gospel stories.

Jesus knew and loved them during his life. They were the people who watched him grow and knew his voice, his face, his walk and all those human traits that only friends and loved ones know.

They sat at the same table and walked the same village streets as Jesus did. Sharing the same human place and time with him, they had a special bond with the Word made flesh. We can hardly know him without knowing them.

They were eyewitnesses of Jesus' life and resurrection from the dead. Many of them died because they told others what they saw and heard. By reason of their testimony, generations of Christians believe in him.

This book tells their stories.

Each of them is a unique witness. Yet Mary of Nazareth is foremost among those who knew Jesus. The bond between Mary and her Son surpassed all others. Blessed by God's grace, she had an unrivaled place in the life of Jesus. For that reason Mary's story is more prominent than any other.

Where can the stories of Jesus' friends be found? Certainly, one must begin with the New Testament. This is what I have done.

Besides the New Testament, I have been helped by the rich background material concerning the times of Jesus that modern historical and cultural studies provide.

Yet saints are not only figures of their own time. They abide with every generation. Christians believe, as the Apostles' Creed teaches, that the saints continue in communion with those who still inhabit this world. "From their place in heaven they guide us still" (Preface of the Apostles). They always have a part in the saving activity of Jesus Christ in the world.

And so I have added stories and traditions about these friends of Jesus that come from later ages, even from our own time. Christians have always seen Mary and Joseph, Peter, James, John and the others as beloved companions. Nations and cities and peoples have felt their rich presence and inspiration. We have a rich legacy of churches, shrines, devotions, stories and art honoring them as patrons and friends. I have drawn from all of these to enhance the text.

My hope is that Christians of today find these great saints their companions, too. For as his friends they inevitably lead others to Jesus himself.

Mary, the Mother of Jesus

Her name was Mary, a form of the name Miriam, the famous sister of Moses. The name was common among Jewish women in those days.

A well-known tradition says Mary was born in Jerusalem, the daughter of Joachim and Ann. Other early sources say Mary was born in Nazareth. There is even an ancient record that points to Sepphoris, a town a few miles from Nazareth, as her birthplace.

Wherever she was born, Mary's life most likely unfolded in the staunch Jewish settlement of Nazareth in the hills of Galilee, not far from the important caravan routes linking Egypt and Mesopotamia.

The Jewish people were strong and robust. The hill climate was dry and healthful and the land often lacked water. No one knew from one year to the next if enough rain would fall or if invading locusts or field mice would spoil the crops. Facing uncertainty only made the people of Galilee more hardworking and close-knit. Struggling for a living deepened their religious spirit. They learned you must depend always on God.

Her Daily Life

Mary was a woman of rural Galilee and most likely lived in a small family house of stone and mud-brick. She worked like any young girl, grinding wheat and barley into flour, preparing dishes of beans, vegetables, eggs, fruit, nuts and occasional chunks of mutton. Wool had to be made into clothing. Bread had to be baked. A few chickens and a donkey had to be fed. And in the village, small as it was, there were always little children to care for.

Almost daily, she carried a large jar of water from the town well for washing and cooking (the well still supplies modern Nazareth today and is called "Mary's Well"). Early on, the Jewish people found that cleanliness prevented disease, so frequent washing, an important chore of women, became part of their religious practice. The well also was a favorite spot where women talked and traded bits of everyday news.

Just as for the other women of Nazareth, the seasons and times of harvest determined what Mary had to do. With the first downpour of rain in October, the vital wheat crop was sown on the mountain fields, to be gathered, if all went well, in May. Small dark olives, knocked from dull green trees in September, had to be pressed into oil for lamps and food. In May or June, early figs were harvested; in July, the softer juicy fruit. Grapes and pomegranates ripened in September and October. God blessed the hills of Galilee with his bounty, but it could never be taken for granted. The unpredictable land could just as well give nothing to those working it.

From the people of Nazareth, Mary learned

11

George Angelini. *Mary Prepares a Meal While Jesus Watches (Contemporary)*

about life. Few strangers visited the town. It had little wealth, culture or learning. But just as a tiny drop of water displays a wealth of organisms, the small town of Nazareth had a rich life of its own. Children were born, young people married, others died and were buried. Mary felt these joys and sorrows. A sheep was lost, a family quarreled, a son left home. From such small things, life's deepest lessons could be learned.

Her Rich Faith

The people of Nazareth had a strong Jewish faith. As God's chosen people, descendants of Abraham, Isaac and Jacob, the Jewish people believed this land was theirs, given to their ancestors whom Moses led out of Egypt. They knew by heart the deeds of kings like David and Solomon and the words of prophets like Isaiah and Elijah. Even though the Romans, with Herod's family as their puppets, now occupied Palestine, the Jews of Galilee believed God would someday send a Messiah who would free Israel from her enemies.

They lived in a war-torn land. For centuries before the Roman occupation, conquering armies of Babylonians, Assyrians, Persians and Greeks fought over Palestine. Despite their wars, revolts and riots, the Jews remained a subject people - taxed, bullied and despised by succeeding rulers.

Like their compatriots, the Jews of Nazareth were never far from the dangers of political violence. During the Jewish uprising in Galilee around 6 A.D., when Jesus was a child, Roman legions captured the city of Sepphoris, five miles from Nazareth, sold all its inhabitants into slavery and burned the city to the ground.

For some Jews, foreign domination only fanned the fires of revolution more brightly in their hearts. Others, like the Pharisees, became more strictly conservative and exclusive in their religious practices. Still others, like Mary and many ordinary people of the land, became more and more aware that they were powerless themselves, but God, the all-powerful, could raise up the lowly. Their faith was of the deepest kind:

> Hear, O Israel: The Lord is our God, the Lord alone. You shall love the Lord your God with all your heart, and with all your soul, and with all your might.
> (Deuteronomy 6:4-5)

Mary's faith was strong. Yet in fervently religious Nazareth with its high moral standards, she hardly stood out at all, even in the eyes of those who knew her best.

When she was fifteen or so, Mary's parents made plans for her to be married, as was customary in those days. They chose Joseph of Nazareth, a carpenter, to be her husband. The engagement took place and Mary returned home to wait about a year before she would go to live with her husband as his wife. But then, something happened:

A Stroke of Lightning

In the sixth month the angel Gabriel was sent by God to a town in Galilee called Nazareth, to a virgin engaged to a man whose name was Joseph, of the house of David. The virgin's name was Mary. And he came to her and said, "Greeting, favored one! The Lord is with you." But she was much perplexed by his words

13

14   Gerard David. *The Annunciation* (15-16th Century)

and pondered what sort of greeting this might be. The angel said to her, "Do not be afraid, Mary, for you have found favor with God. And now, you will conceive in your womb and bear a son, and you will name him Jesus. He will be great and will be called the Son of the Most High, and the Lord God will give him the throne of his ancestor David. He will reign over the house of Jacob forever, and of his kingdom there will be no end." Mary said to the angel, "How can this be, since I am a virgin?" The angel said to her, "The Holy Spirit will come upon you, and the power of the Most High will overshadow you; therefore the child to be born will be holy; he will be called Son of God. And now, your relative Elizabeth in her old age has also conceived a son; and this is the sixth month for her who was said to be barren. For nothing is impossible with God." Then Mary said, "Here I am, the servant of the Lord; let it be with me according to your word." Then the angel departed from her.

(Luke 1:26-38)

The gospels, compiled years after these events at Nazareth, tell the story of Jesus and recall Mary only incidentally. True, St. Luke's account sees Mary favored by God, the Lord's handmaid, a model believer. His story describes her fear and perplexity, her faith and acceptance during the angel's visit. But still, we are left to ourselves to imagine Mary's life and her experience when the angel left her.

The angel's message struck like lightning, changing everything for her. Immense joy filled the young girl's soul when she conceived the child by the power of the Holy Spirit. But when the angel left, Mary was alone.

Living with Mystery

Nazareth certainly was unaware of the angel's visit. That day and the days afterward, men tended the fields, the aroma of fresh bread filled the village air and women talked around the well. The Word of God was made flesh, but the people of Nazareth saw nothing changed. In their eyes Mary was still a young girl of sixteen espoused to Joseph the carpenter.

Once the angel left, Mary faced some troubling questions with only faith to guide her. What about her marriage to Joseph? Since she was bearing a child that was not his, Mary had to face the anguishing prospect of divorce and the shame it could bring down upon her in a small town that frowned on an unfaithful wife. Even though he had a high regard for her, how could she explain to Joseph the mysterious act of God and an angel no one else saw?

The threat was removed when an angel appeared to Joseph in a dream and said: "Joseph, son of David, do not be afraid to take Mary home as your wife, because she has conceived by the Holy Spirit. She will give birth to a son and you must name him Jesus."

When Joseph awakened, he took Mary as his wife to his home. Together they would do what God would have them do.

Mary Visits Her Cousin

Three months after the angel's annunciation,

Rogier van der Weyden. *The Visitation* (15th Century)

Mary visited her relative Elizabeth, the elderly wife of Zachary who served as a priest in the Temple at Jerusalem. Mary had been told that this couple advanced in age was to have a child, too, "for nothing is impossible with God."

In those days Mary set out and went with haste to a Judean town in the hill country, where she entered the house of Zechariah and greeted Elizabeth. When Elizabeth heard Mary's greeting, the child leaped in her womb. And Elizabeth was filled with the Holy Spirit and exclaimed with a loud cry, "Blessed are you among women, and blessed is the fruit of your womb. And why has this happened to me, that the mother of my Lord comes to me? For as soon as I heard the sound of your greeting, the child in my womb leaped for joy. And blessed is she who believed that there would be a fulfillment of what was spoken to her by the Lord."

(Luke 1:39–45)

Mary stayed with Elizabeth for about three months and then went back home. Finally, six months later her own son was born.

Her Child Is Born

In those days a decree went out from Emperor Augustus that all the world should be registered. This was the first registration and was taken while Quirinius was governor of Syria. All went to their own towns to be registered. Joseph also went from the town of Nazareth in Galilee to Judea, to the city of David called Bethlehem, because he was descended from the house and family of David. He went to be registered with Mary, to whom he was engaged and who was expecting a child. While they were there, the time came for her to deliver her child. And she gave birth to her firstborn son and wrapped him in bands of cloth, and laid him in a manger, because there was no place for them in the inn. In that region there were shepherds living in the fields, keeping watch over their flock by night. Then an angel of the Lord stood before them, and the glory of the Lord shone around them, and they were terrified. But the angel said to them, "Do not be afraid; for see - I am bringing you good news of great joy for all the people: to you is born this day in the city of David a Savior, who is the Messiah, the Lord. This will be a sign for you: you will find a child wrapped in bands of cloth and lying in a manger." And suddenly there was with the angel a multitude of the heavenly host, praising God and saying,

Attributed to Gerard David. *The Adoration of the Magi* (15-16th Century)

"Glory to God in the highest heaven, and on earth peace among those whom he favors!" When the angels had left them and gone into heaven, the shepherds said to one another, "Let us go now to Bethlehem and see this thing that has taken place, which the Lord has made known to us." So they went with haste and found Mary and Joseph, and the child lying in the manger. When they saw this, they made known what had been told them about this child; and all who heard it were amazed at what the shepherds told them. But Mary treasured all these words and pondered them in her heart. The shepherds returned,

glorifying and praising God for all they had heard and seen, as it had been told them.

(Luke 2:1-20)

Prophecies in the Temple

After the birth of Jesus, according to St. Luke's Gospel, Mary and Joseph fulfilled what Jewish law customarily required when a child was born. Eight days later, they had the child circumcised and gave him the name Jesus.

After forty days, they took him to the Temple at Jerusalem to consecrate him to God. There, the old man Simeon and the old woman Anna recognized the child's extraordinary mission.

Taking him into his arms, Simeon said to Mary the mother: "You see this child: he is destined for the fall and for the rising of many in Israel, destined to be a sign that is rejected, and a sword shall pierce your own soul, too, so that the secrets of many hearts may be laid bare."

Then they returned to Galilee, to their own town of Nazareth.

Visit of the Magi

St. Matthew, however, describes less tranquil circumstances following the birth of Christ. When Jesus was born in Bethlehem, Magi from the east arrived to pay him homage, guided by a star. Seeking information of the child's whereabouts from King Herod, they found Jesus with Mary his mother. They offered gifts of gold, frankincense and myrrh. Then, warned of Herod's purpose to kill the child, they departed quickly for their own country by another route.

Cosimo di Turo. *Flight into Egypt* (15th Century)

The Escape to Egypt

"Rise, take the child and his mother," the angel said to Joseph. "Flee to Egypt and stay there till I tell you."

Safe in Mary's arms, Jesus was taken into Egypt where he escaped Herod's massacre of the innocent children of Bethlehem. When, at the angel's command, the child returned to his own land, he had relived the ancient journey of Israel, the Exodus.

Both Matthew and Luke suddenly end their accounts of Jesus' early days when he settled with his family at Nazareth. Except for St. Luke's story of the pilgrimage of the boy Jesus to Jerusalem, the gospels are silent about Jesus and Mary until his public life begins.

Jesus Missing for Three Days

St. Luke relates the story of one pilgrimage the holy family took to Jerusalem:

Every year his parents used to go to Jerusalem

for the feast of Passover. When he was twelve years old, they went for the feast as usual.

When they were on their way home after the feast, the boy Jesus stayed behind in Jerusalem without his parents' knowledge. They assumed he was with the caravan, and it was only after a day's journey that they went to look for him among their relations and acquaintances. When they failed to find him, they went back to Jerusalem, looking for him everywhere.

Three days later, they found him in the Temple, sitting among the doctors, listening to them and asking questions; and all those who heard him were astounded at his intelligence and his answers.

They were overcome when they saw him, and his mother said to him, "My child, why have you done this to us? See how worried your father and I have been, looking for you."

"Why were you looking for me?" he replied. "Did you not know that I must be busy with my Father's affairs?" But they did not understand what he meant.

He then went down with them and came to Nazareth and lived under their authority. His mother stored up all these things in her heart, and Jesus increased in wisdom and stature and grew in favor with God and men.

The Silent Years

His long years at Nazareth are called his "hidden life," the years he grew in "wisdom and age and grace," the years with Mary and Joseph. Nazareth was his first and only school; Mary and Joseph his principal teachers. From them, the Son of God learned to speak his first words, in the accent of Galilee. They acquainted him with the ways of the village and the ways of the human heart. Before anyone else, he listened to and learned from Joseph and Mary.

They taught him to appreciate familiar things from the Galilean hills; the sower, the shepherd and his sheep, the vineyard, the fig tree. These are the images he later used to convey his deepest thoughts.

Ordinary experiences, like watching Mary place a small measure of yeast into flour and seeing it rise before baking, gave him early images to describe the remarkable ways the kingdom of God touches all things.

He learned the skills of carpentry and the discipline of hard work at Joseph's side. Joseph, Mary and Jesus seldom went beyond their village and the neighboring fields. Their home was one simple room, used for work by day and as a bedroom by night. There were openings in the limestone floor which fed into grain silos that were carved for storage out of the rock below; on the wall, a niche for an oil lamp, the only light in the windowless room. On summer days, a shelter of branches shaded the flat roof above.

Though Jerusalem was the center of Jewish worship, the Jewish people of Galilee made the eighty-mile journey to the Temple only for the great pilgrimage feasts of Passover, Pentecost and Tabernacles. Their faith was nourished in their home and in the local synagogue. There at Nazareth, Jesus grew to know his own Jewish traditions.

After the Death of Joseph

Joseph's death, some years before Jesus' public ministry, left Mary a widow, depending more than ever on her Son for support.

Devoted to him, she knew he had a

mysterious, divine role. Yet, in those long years at Nazareth, she had no heavenly signs to go by. No angel spoke to her; no witnesses came forward to explain anything more of her child's destiny.

At Nazareth Jesus was her faithful Son, working at his trade, following the seasons and the harvests, hardly noticed by his neighbors and relatives. Mary was his mother.

Mary's Imprint on Jesus

It would be natural that Mary's imprint appear in Jesus' later teachings. The way he valued childhood and family life surely came from rich memories of home life at Nazareth and its simplicity, trust and love.

His later parables and teachings show his esteem for the faith and patience of women and condemn the injustices done to them in the male-dominated society of his time. His advocacy and appreciation for women surely followed his love and respect for the woman who was his mother. He was sensitive to the plight of widows. Surely he was influenced by Mary's situation after the death of Joseph.

Was Jesus' love for his own religious tradition and his ability to be critical of that tradition fostered by the honest sense and devotion of a woman like Mary and a man like Joseph? One thing is certain: Nazareth left an imprint on his experience.

Her Son Leaves Home

When he was about thirty, Jesus left Nazareth to stay for awhile in the desert of Judea near the River Jordan where John the Baptist was preaching and baptizing. People said that a prophet had arisen in Israel and that God was speaking in that lonely place.

Christ Taking Leave of His Mother. 16th Century.

As she watched her Son go, Mary sensed that the long years of silence were coming to an end.

In those days Jesus came from Nazareth of Galilee and was baptized by John in the Jordan . . . Now after John was arrested, Jesus came to Galilee, proclaiming the good news of God, and saying, "The time has come near; repent, and believe in the good news."

(Mark 1:9, 14-15)

He preached in the synagogues around Capernaum on the Lake of Galilee, healing the sick and driving out evil spirits from those who were afflicted. Great crowds flocked to him.

But when he went up to Nazareth, he was rejected. "Where did this man get all this?"

they said when he spoke in their synagogue. "Is he not the carpenter, the son of Mary...?"

"A prophet is not without honor except in his native place and among his own relations and in his own house," Jesus replied, amazed at their lack of faith. He left Nazareth and never returned.

Sees Her Son Rejected

His rejection by his own people undoubtedly caused Mary deep sorrow. She sided with her Son when even some of his own relations thought he had gone mad and wanted to seize him. The old man Simeon had predicted in the Temple when Mary had presented her infant that he would be rejected by his own people.

We don't know where Mary lived during the time of Jesus' public ministry. At Nazareth with some relatives? Or did she move to Capernaum to live among his disciples? Wherever she was, she did not have Jesus as close to her as before.

Jesus' eyes now turned to a larger family.

And he replied, "Who are my mother and my brothers?" And looking at those around him, he said, "Here are my mother and my brothers! Whoever does the will of God is my brother and sister and mother."

(Mark 3:33-35)

Quietly Following Her Son

Mary had no prominent place in the ministry of Jesus. She was rarely with him.

True, according to John's Gospel, she prompted his first miracle at a wedding feast in Cana of Galilee when he turned water into wine. "Do whatever he tells you," she said to the stewards at the banquet.

Mary mostly remained at a distance while others told her what he said and did. If she had a role during his ministry, it was that of a believer, treasuring in her heart what she heard and trying to understand the meaning of it all. Later, a more active part would be hers.

She followed her Son from afar as he traveled through Galilee to Jerusalem.

"Blessed is the womb that bore you and the breasts that nursed you," some shouted as he passed. And Mary rejoiced at their praise. But she also knew he had powerful enemies whose threats and plots to destroy him increased every day.

When Jesus and his disciples went up to Jerusalem to celebrate the Passover, Mary followed him too, with some relatives and friends. She knew danger awaited them there.

With Her Son as He Dies

And this is what the soldiers did. Meanwhile, standing near the cross of Jesus were his mother, and his mother's sister, Mary the wife of Clopas, and Mary Magdalene.

(John 19:25)

We can hardly guess how Mary experienced the tragic days when they arrested and crucified her Son.

Tradition says she stood on the road as Jesus passed by carrying his cross. When all his disciples fled, she remained with him. Helpless to do anything else, she watched her dying Son and offered her love.

When he died, they took him down from

the cross and placed him in her arms. She held him gently, her child of long ago.

Her Joy

She was one of those who saw him risen from the dead. Her cries of grief turned into cries of joy as she waited in prayer with the apostles for the Holy Spirit that Jesus promised to send them.

As the mother of Jesus, Mary had a special place among his followers, strengthening their faith through her own. From his cross, Jesus gave her to his church as a mother for all ages.

We do not know for sure the place or circumstances of Mary's death. One strong tradition attests that she died in Jerusalem. Another tradition points to the city of Ephesus, where she is said to have lived for a while with the apostle John.

MARY IN CHRISTIAN TRADITION
The Scriptures: First Century

But when the fullness of time had come, God sent his Son, born of a woman, born under the law.
(Galatians 4:4)

Except for this reference, Mary is not mentioned in the earliest Christian writings, the letters of St. Paul. Only the four gospels, written between 65 and 100 A.D., speak of her at any length.

Mark and Luke

Mark's Gospel carries only a brief reference to Mary. It says simply that Jesus is "the son of Mary," omitting any details of his birth or family life. For Mark, belief in Jesus is more

El Greco. *Pentecost* (17th Century)

important than to have ties of flesh and blood with him. This gospel praises Mary as a believer who does the will of God (Mk 3:31-35) and is a true disciple of her Son.

In Luke's beautiful, extended narration of

Filippo Lippi. *The Virgin, the Infant Jesus, and Saint John.* (15th Century)

And Mary said, "My soul magnifies the Lord, and my spirit rejoices in God my Savior, for he has looked with favor on the lowliness of his servant. Surely, from now on all generations will call me blessed."

(Luke 1:46-48)

Matthew and John

Matthew's Gospel, intent on tracing Jesus' descent as the Messiah from David through Joseph, presents Mary less prominently than Luke. Matthew, however, strongly insists on Mary's unique virginal conception: "...before they lived together she was with child through the Holy Spirit" (Mt 1:18). Later, this belief in her virginal conception would bring Mary an honored title, the Mother of God.

John's Gospel, the last of the four, speaks twice of Mary. At Cana in Galilee she intercedes with her Son for a newly married couple and he changes water into wine (Jn 2:1-12). On Calvary she stands beneath the cross at Jesus' death (Jn 19:25-27). The stories of Cana and Calvary led generations of Christians to go to Mary in their need and to rely on her compassion in their suffering.

At Cana and on Calvary Jesus calls his mother "Woman," which early Christian tradition saw as an allusion likening Mary to the first woman, Eve. In God's plan, Mary's faithful response to the angel reversed the failure of Eve, and she became the new "mother of all the living."

Later Christian devotion to Mary was nourished primarily by what the four gospels said of her. But other factors, too, contributed to the development of Christian feeling and piety toward the mother of Jesus.

the events surrounding the birth of Christ, Mary appears as "the handmaid of the Lord." Drawing, probably, on the devotion of early Jewish-Christians who saw the mother of Jesus as a faithful Israelite living the ordinary life of "the people of the land," Luke portrays her as a woman of grace, responding to God's mysterious overtures with firm trust and acceptance. Though she questions and does not all together understand God's plan presented by the angel, she believes.

"Be it done to me according to your word," Mary's response to the angel's invitation, is the response every Christian must make in order to transform the events of life and receive God's blessing.

MARY IN EARLY POPULAR CHRISTIAN LITERATURE

Popular Christian stories about Christ, Mary and the apostles, originating in Syria, Palestine and Egypt from the mid-second century, greatly influenced the way ordinary Christians imagined Mary's life. These stories, attempting to supply details omitted in the gospels, went beyond and sometimes contrary to the indications of the scriptures.

The "Gospel of James," one of these stories written about 150 A.D., portrays the childhood of Mary in this way:

When Mary was one year old, Joachim made a great feast and invited the priest and scribes, and the whole people of Israel assembled. And Joachim brought the child to the priests, and they blessed her saying: O God of our fathers, bless this child and give her a name renowned forever among all generations. And all the people said: "So be it, so be it. Amen..." And the child became three years old, and Joachim said: "Call the virgin daughters of the Hebrews and let them accompany the child to the Temple of the Lord with lamps burning in their hands." And they went up to the temple of the Lord. And the priests received her and kissed her and blessed her, saying: "The Lord has magnified your name among all generations; in you the Lord will show redemption to the children of Israel." And he sat her on the third step of the altar. And the Lord gave her grace and she danced with her feet and all the house of the Lord loved her. And her parents returned home marveling and praising the Lord because their child did not turn back. And Mary was in the temple of the Lord to be nurtured like a dove; and she received food from the hand of an angel.

By presenting Mary as a sheltered virgin absorbed in serving God in the Temple from her youth, the story sought to defend Christian belief in the virgin birth. Mary lived a protected life before her marriage to Joseph. Yet, unfortunately, the story removed Mary from the ordinary, uneventful village life that scripture suggests was hers.

The account offers details of Mary's marriage to Joseph, who is portrayed as an old widower with his own children, and relates further wonders that accompanied the birth of Jesus in a cave. This early story, which powerfully affected the imagination of Christians, has left its mark on Christian art, liturgy and devotion.

Early Churches and Feasts of Mary

Prompted by this story, in the fifth century a church was built in Jerusalem close by the Temple site honoring Mary's birthplace and home. The ancient church of St. Ann, the mother of Mary, stands on that place today.

The Feasts of the Immaculate Conception (Dec. 8), the Birth of Mary (Sept. 8) and the Presentation of Mary in the Temple (Nov. 21), which are celebrated by many of the Christian churches of the East and West, were also influenced by this popular story.

The Feast of the Dormition of the Mother of God is celebrated August 15th. The Icon of the Dormition represents the Virgin lying on her death bed, surrounded by the apostles, with Christ in glory receiving her soul into his arms.

Mary's Death and Assumption into Heaven

Stories from the fifth century (or perhaps earlier) recount Mary's later life, her death and assumption into heaven, events unreported by the four gospels.

The legends describe Jesus appearing to Mary in the house on Mount Sion in Jerusalem where she lived after Pentecost. Her Son tells her she is soon to die. Then from all parts of the world the apostles gather to bid her farewell:

> Stretching out his hands the Lord received her holy soul. And when her soul departed, the place was filled with a sweet smell and bright light. And a voice from heaven proclaimed: "Blessed are you among women." Peter and John, Paul and Thomas, ran to embrace her feet and receive her holiness; and the twelve apostles took her body on a bier and bore it forth. Instructed by Jesus, Peter and the other apostles took her body to be buried in a new tomb near Gethsemane in the Kidron Valley, where miracles of healing accompanied her burial. Three days later, angels took her body to heaven.
> (Ps John:The Dormition of Mary, 4th c.)

By the year 600, a feast called the Dormition of Mary, honoring her death and assumption into heaven, was celebrated in Jerusalem and in the churches of the East. Some centuries later it would pass into the Western churches, known as the Feast of the Assumption of Mary.

Early Palestinian Shrines Honoring Mary

Besides these early stories, devotion to Mary was nourished by the honor paid to certain ancient sites in Palestine associated with Jesus and his mother:

- At Bethlehem, the grotto of Christ's birth was held sacred.
- At the Mount of Olives outside Jerusalem, grottoes recalling his agony in the garden and ascension were frequented by early Jewish Christians. Mary's grave, too, was honored in this area.
- At Jerusalem, the sites where Jesus died and was buried were remembered.
- On Mount Sion in Jerusalem, the early 25

church met for worship on the site where the Holy Spirit came upon Mary and the disciples at Pentecost.

• At Nazareth, the sites of Jesus' early life were remembered.

Even when Roman armies laid waste to much of Palestine in 70 A.D. and again after the Jewish revolts of 132-135 A.D., Palestinian Christians kept alive the memories and traditions of these holy places where Mary was honored along with her Son.

The Christian "Holy Land" of the Fourth Century

After the Emperor Constantine accepted Christianity in 313 A.D., he set about making Palestine a vital Christian center of the Roman empire. Under his direction, great churches and shrines were built on the ancient sites of the holy places and Palestine became a land of Christian pilgrimage, a visual gospel.

From 335 A.D. onward, Christian pilgrims from all over the empire, bishops, priests and lay people, flocked to the Holy Land. They wanted to see the manger, the wood of the cross, anything that survived from Jesus' time. Praying at the sacred sites and other shrines, their faith was strengthened. Relics (sometimes authentic, sometimes not) were offered for their devotion. Returning home with their memories and with relics and souvenirs, they celebrated the feasts and sacred places they experienced in the Holy Land in their own liturgies, churches and shrines.

Mary, the mother of Jesus, had a special role in their experience. Her presence in the Holy Land seemed to be everywhere. Devotion to her was nourished by the experience of pilgrimage.

Medieval Devotion to Mary

The Christian people of the Middle Ages suffered constantly from disease, famine and wars which they were helpless to do anything about. They turned anxiously to Mary for assistance. Their faith led them to trust her to intercede for them with her Son as she did for the ordinary people at the marriage feast of Cana.

Our Lady of Vladimir. The tenderness of Mary is captured in this 12th-century Byzantine icon revered by Russian Christians.

Since she was a compassionate mother who experienced the sufferings of Calvary, they petitioned her for cures from sickness, for protection and help. Her kindness and power were proclaimed everywhere; in the sermons they heard, in art and song and prayer.

Meditating on the Life of Mary

Popular classics like "The Meditations on the Life of Christ", a book dating from the thirteenth century, nourished medieval devotion to Mary.

Widely circulated, it taught Christians to see the lives of Jesus and Mary through a "pilgrimage of the imagination." By meditating on the stories of the gospel, embellished with additional details and legends, one could enter into the world of Christ and his saints and learn from them how to live.

Stories from the Meditations, appealing and tender as the following short excerpt from "The Nativity of Jesus" shows, greatly influenced the way medieval Christians saw Mary and also inspired the works of so many medieval artists.

...the emperor wrote a proclamation that the whole world should be registered, and everyone go to his own city. So obeying the command, Joseph started on his way with our Lady, taking with him an ox and an ass, since she was pregnant and the road was five miles long from Bethlehem to Jerusalem. They arrived like poor owners of animals. Now they could not find an inn when they arrived at Bethlehem, because they were poor and many others were there to register, too. Pity our Lady, and see this delicate girl, only 15 years old, as she walks so carefully, tired by the journey and jostled by the crowds. They were sent away by everyone, the childlike mother and the old man, Joseph, her husband. When they saw an empty cave that people used when it rained, they entered it for shelter. And Joseph, who was an expert carpenter, probably closed it in some way...When Jesus was born Mary wrapped him in the veil from her head and laid him in a manger. The ox and the ass knelt with their mouths above the manger and breathed on the infant as if they knew the child was poorly clothed and needed to be warmed in that cold season. The mother also knelt to adore him and to thank God, saying: "I thank you, Father, that you gave me your Son and I adore you, eternal God, my son." Joseph also adored him. Then Joseph took the ass's saddle and pulled out the stuffing of straw and placed it near the manger so our Lady might rest on it. She sat down and stayed there, her face turned constantly toward the manger, her eyes fixed lovingly on her dear Son.

Mary, the Mother of God: 431 A.D.

Religious controversy also stimulated devotion to Mary in the early church. In 431, the Council of Ephesus repudiated Nestorius, the patriarch of Constantinople, for refusing to honor Mary with the title "Mother of God." Orthodox believers held to the title because it safeguarded Christian belief in the mystery of the Incarnation: Jesus is God and man.

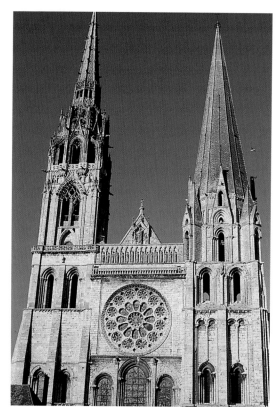

The Cathedral at Chartres, France which was dedicated to Mary in the 12th century.

especially in the churches of the East, where they became objects of special devotion.

Europe as a Holy Land: 11th - 15th Centuries

The Muslim conquest of Palestine in the seventh century brought the holy places under non-Christian rule that became increasingly hostile toward Christian pilgrims. When the Turks threatened the ancient Christian shrines with destruction, the Christian nations of Europe sought to reconquer the Holy Land in the Crusades of the eleventh century.

During these disturbed times, when pilgrimage was drastically curtailed, the shrines and relics of Palestine were duplicated or transferred to the countries of Europe. In Spain, France, England, Italy, Germany and the Lowlands, great medieval shrines like those in the Holy Land arose in places like Chartres, Monserrat, Walsinham and Loretto. This "European Holy Land" became the setting for the early medieval Christian's devotion to the Mother of God.

In a way similar to this, Christian visionaries, mystics and writers recounted their experience of the gospel stories. The "revelations" of St. Bridgit of Sweden (1303-1373), as well as many popular stories of the gospel, are examples of this meditative approach to the scripture. They influenced Christian devotion to Mary.

The Protestant Reformation

The Protestant reformers of the sixteenth century attacked the low standards that began to harm European devotion to Mary in late medieval times. They condemned superstitious practices exaggerating Mary's power and

The church did not seek to make Mary a goddess, otherwise she could not have given birth to Christ as someone truly human. She could be called Mother of God, however, because Jesus who was born from her truly was Son of God for all eternity.

Popular feeling for Mary ran high in the Christian world after the Council, and churches dedicated to her arose in almost every important city. In the city of Constantinople, an important center of devotion to Mary, 250 churches and shrines in her honor were built before the eighth century. Pictures and icons of Mary holding her divine Child multiplied, position, some of which seemed to place her above Christ himself.

Yet Luther or Calvin never rejected veneration of Mary totally. They saw her as a model whose humble faith Christians could imitate. The reformers, however, discouraged Marian pilgrimages and shrines, suppressed her feasts and forbade prayers for her intercession.

The Catholic Church, while acknowledging abuses to Mary, upheld the privileges and practices which longstanding Christian tradition accorded her as the Mother of Jesus.

Catholic Devotion to Mary from the Reformation to Today

Within the Catholic world of Europe and America, devotion to Mary flourished from the seventeenth century until the time of the Second Vatican Council in the twentieth century. Devotion to Mary during this time strongly influenced every aspect of Roman Catholic culture and piety. Among Eastern and Orthodox Christians also, devotion to Mary continued to be strong.

In the Western church, numerous religious communities and societies, such as the Oblates of Mary Immaculate, the Marists, the Sisters of Notre Dame and the Legion of Mary, were founded under her patronage. They sought to imitate Mary's motherly concern to bring the message of her Son to all peoples through their work in schools, hospitals and missions throughout the world.

Apparitions of Mary

In the nineteenth and twentieth centuries, apparitions of Mary reported in Lourdes (1858) in France, Knock (1879) in Ireland, Fatima (1917) in Portugal and other places

Our Lady of Guadalupe. 16th Century. This picture hangs in the Basilica of our Lady of Guadalupe in Mexico City.

created widespread interest among Catholics throughout the world. Mary, appearing to people who were mostly uneducated, often only children, called for worldwide repentance and a renewal of faith in her Son.

Many ordinary people suffering from the poverty created by the Industrial Revolution and the destructiveness of modern warfare saw these apparitions of Mary as a sign from heaven that God still cared for his people.

Miracles of healing were reported at these shrines, which became new popular centers of devotion to the Mother of God.

Traditional Marian shrines such as Guadalupe in Mexico and Our Lady of

Czestochowa in Poland continued to be rallying places and political influences in their nations and among their people.

The Story of Our Lady of Guadalupe

Just before dawn on December 9, 1531, ten years after the Spanish conquest of Mexico, Juan Diego, an Aztec Indian, was walking from his village in the country to catechism instruction and Mass at the Franciscan center in Mexico City.

As he approached the little hill called Tepeyec outside the city, he heard the songs of many different birds echoing in the hills. So beautiful was the sound that he said to himself: "I must be dreaming. It's just like paradise."

He looked eastward, above the hill, where the song seemed to come from. Suddenly, it stopped and there was silence.

Then a voice called to him from the hilltop: "Little Juan, little Juan Diego."

The Indian climbed the hill to see who it was.

As he reached the top he saw a young lady standing there who told him to come closer. Yet when he drew near he was almost blinded by the brightness of her clothes.

The rock she stood on sparkled like a rainbow. The brush on the ground nearby shone like emeralds and the thornbushes were like painted gold.

Juan Diego bowed before her, but her voice was so gentle and courteous that he found himself completely delighted.

"Little Juan, my little child, where are you going?"

"My Lady," he replied, "I'm going to church in the city to learn what holy things the priests of our Lord will tell me."

Her Message

Then she spoke to him and told him this:

"Now listen, my smallest child, I am Mary, the Virgin Mother of God, the Creator of heaven and earth, who gives us life. I wish a shrine to be built for me here, so that I can offer all my love, my compassion, and my protection. For I am your merciful mother - yours, and your neighbors in the land, and all who love me and confide in me. I want to listen when you are grieving and comfort you in sorrow and pain.

"Now, go to the palace of the bishop in Mexico City and tell him my desire to have a shrine built here. Tell him what I have said. Go quickly, my son, my little child."

Juan Diego shows the image of Mary, the Mother of God, to Bishop Zumarrago.

Juan Diego promptly bowed and said: "My Lady, I am your servant. I'll go as you say."

When the Indian arrived at Bishop Zumarrago's palace, he was kept waiting a good while before he saw the bishop. And when he told his story, the bishop listened kindly enough, but was hardly convinced.

"My son, come back when I am not so busy. Let me think about it."

So Juan Diego left, sure that he had failed, and returned to the hillside where the Lady awaited him.

"My Lady, I tried but I failed. I told him what you said. He listened kindly, but he wasn't really convinced. I'm sure he thought I made up the story myself. Now if you want a shrine built here, why don't you send somebody important with your message, somebody famous? Not me. I'm just a little fellow, an ordinary person, a little leaf on a tree. You sent the wrong person."

To Ask for a Sign

But the Lady insisted and sent Juan Diego back again. Eventually, the bishop began to wonder if there were not something behind his story. So he told the Indian to ask the Lady for a sign.

Now, as Juan Diego was returning, someone from his village met him with the news that his uncle was very sick with a burning fever.

Forgetting everything else, he went to his uncle's house, bringing a doctor. But nothing the doctor did could cure him.

"Go to the city and get a priest," his uncle gasped.

Juan Diego started back to the city.

He decided, though, not to go near the hill where he met the Lady, for he did not want to delay. So he went another way, only to be met on the road by his mysterious friend.

"My son, where are you going?" she asked with a smile.

"My uncle is dying," Juan replied anxiously. "Please wait until tomorrow and I'll do as you ask."

"Your uncle is well at home now. Don't worry," the Lady assured him. And, greatly relieved, Juan Diego told her about the bishop's request for a sign.

The Flowers

The Lady directed him to climb the hill where he would find all kinds of flowers and pick them and bring them back to her.

Flowers are rare in December and hardly found in the wild hills. But when Juan climbed the hill he found it covered with fragrant roses of every kind.

He picked them, wrapped them in his poor mantle and carried them to the Lady.

She took them in her hands, carefully arranged them in his mantle again and told him to bring them to the bishop as a sign.

Once more, the Indian, carrying his precious sign, came before the bishop and told him the story.

"Here are the roses," he said, opening his mantle.

As the flowers dropped to the floor, there suddenly appeared on his mantle the image of Mary, the Mother of God, as it is seen today in the church at Guadalupe.

The Story of Our Lady of Lourdes

One of the most famous apparitions of Mary reported in modern times took place at

Since 1858, the Miraculous Grotto at Lourdes, France, has been a popular place of Christian pilgrimage.

Lourdes, a small village in southwest France at the foot of the Pyrenees mountains. Between February 11 and July 16, 1858, the Blessed Virgin appeared eighteen times to a poor fourteen-year-old girl, Bernadette Soubirous.

The appearances began on February 11 as the young girl was gathering firewood with some friends along the bank of the River Gave.

A beautiful Lady appeared to Bernadette from a nearby grotto.

"She looked like a girl of sixteen or seventeen," Bernadette reported. "She was dressed in a white robe fastened at the waist with a blue sash. On her head she wore a white veil, falling almost to her feet which were covered partly by her dress, partly by yellow roses. On her right arm there hung a rosary with white beads on a golden chain that shone like the roses at her feet. She was alert, young and surrounded by light."

Fifteen Days

"Will you come back here for fifteen days?" the Lady asked Bernadette.

The young girl went back despite the opposition and ridicule she suffered from many townspeople when they heard her story.

Sometimes the Lady said nothing, but simply smiled while Bernadette knelt, absorbed by her beauty. At other appearances she spoke of different things and made certain requests.

"Pray to God for sinners," the Lady said to Bernadette on her sixth visit, as she looked at the crowd that accompanied the young girl.

Tears began to fall from Bernadette's eyes.

"I cried because the Lady did," she said.

The Water

The tenth appearance was perhaps the most dramatic.

Inside the grotto, the Lady pointed to the ground and said to the girl, "Go drink at the spring and wash in it."

Bernadette began to dig with her hands in

The Basilica at Lourdes, France, was built near the spring where Saint Bernadette Soubirous reported her visions of the Blessed Mother in 1858.

Filippo Lippi. *The Virgin of the Nativity* (15th Century)

the muddy ground and wash her face with it. Many of those watching her thought she had gone mad. Gradually, a spring of clear water began to flow from that spot.

A few days later, Louis Brouillette, a wagon driver who had lost his sight in an accident, regained it after washing in the water.

The tradition of healing associated with Lourdes began with that incident.

On March 1, Bernadette took a friend's rosary to the grotto and began to say it when the Lady appeared.

"Don't you have a rosary of your own?" the Blessed Virgin asked. "Use that."

On March 2, the Lady suggested that the people make a procession to the grotto and told Bernadette to tell the priests to build a chapel there, even a small one.

But the girl was strongly rebuked by her parish priest.

On March 3, several thousand people crowded before the grotto, but Bernadette did not see the Lady until late evening. She had not come earlier, the Lady explained, because the people had come merely out of curiosity.

Her Answer

On March 25, the Feast of the Annunciation, Bernadette woke up early and went to the grotto at Massabielle around 4 o'clock. Until then, she had never asked her visitor who she was.

"I don't know if it is the Blessed Virgin," she had said to those who inquired. "It is a beautiful Lady."

"My Lady," Bernadette asked when the apparition appeared, "will you tell me who you are?"

"I am the Immaculate Conception," the Lady answered.

The great shrine of Lourdes, which attracts millions of pilgrims each year from all over the world, honors these apparitions. Today, it is probably the most popular shrine honoring Mary.

Its statue of Mary (of which Bernadette is said to have exclaimed, "It's not like her; the difference is like day and night!", is duplicated in countless Roman Catholic churches and homes.

The Second Vatican Council

The Second Vatican Council, in its Constitution on the Church (Lumen Gentium), summed up the church's belief about Mary and devotion to her:

We turn our eyes to Mary, a model for all believers. Faithfully meditating on her and contemplating her in light of the Word made man, the church enters more intimately into the great mystery of the Incarnation.

For Mary unites in herself the great teachings of faith, and so she calls believers to her Son and his sacrifice and to the love of the Father.

Seeking the glory of Christ, the church becomes more like her and progresses in faith, hope and love, seeking and doing the will of God in all things...

Just as the Mother of Jesus, glorified in body and soul in heaven, is the image and beginning of the church as it is to be perfected in the world to come, so, too, does she shine forth on earth, until the day the Lord comes. as a sign of sure hope and solace to the People of God during its sojourn on earth. (L.G. 65, 68)

Joseph

He was known as Joseph, son of Jacob, to the people in the town of Nazareth in Galilee's southern hills.

Outside of Narareth he was called Joseph of Nazareth, the carpenter.

His name and the town where he lived might never be known today except for Jesus Christ. Jesus, the Son of God, spent almost thirty years of his life in Nazareth.

Nazareth

No one knows when people first settled in the secluded basin in the rocky Galilean hills above the fertile lands of the Great Plain. The hill country around Nazareth hardly welcomed a town at all. Its only resource was a spring of good water which probably drew people to the spot first and kept them there.

By hard work they cleared the ground for small plots where crops and vines could grow. By the time of Jesus, Nazareth, with its few hundred people, was a town of small farms and vineyards - nothing more.

The people of Nazareth were all religious Jews devoted to their traditions and their synagogue. Outsiders said they were simple and uncultured, somewhat out of step with the world beyond their hill town.

Nathaniel, one of Jesus' future apostles, summed up the opinion most people had of the place: "Can anything good come from Nazareth?"

But the Nazareans preferred their life apart.

Rather than live on more choice land next to gentile neighbors, as Jews did in so many other towns in Galilee, or in prosperous Greek cities like Tiberias on the Lake of Galilee, they chose the remote hills where they could live as Jews without interference from outsiders.

Joseph the Carpenter

Joseph was the carpenter of Nazareth. Not only did he make tools and furniture out of wood, but he probably built and repaired his neighbors' simple houses and sheds.

Occasionally he may have left his town to work elsewhere on projects that needed skilled laborers like him. For in those days, Herod Antipas, the ambitious ruler of Galilee, was constantly constructing new buildings, even new cities, throughout the region and good workers were always in demand.

Later Joseph may even have taken his young son along to work at his side.

Each year as many of the people of Nazareth as could do so made the four-day journey to Jerusalem, the holy city, to celebrate

George Angelini. *Joseph, with Jesus at his side, working at his carpenter's bench (Contemporary)*

Nazareth, where Jesus was raised. (Photo early 1900's)

the Jewish feasts. There they were easily recognized as Galileans by their way of speaking and their rough clothes and manners. But few people had even heard of Nazareth or could tell you where it was.

"Upright" Hopeful Man

The gospel calls Joseph an "upright" man.

He was upright because, like his neighbors at Nazareth, he observed all the Jewish laws.

But not from lip service.

Joseph firmly believed in his heart in the God of Israel, who loved all things great and small, yes, even Nazareth and a humble carpenter.

An inward man, Joseph saw in the simple, ordinary world about him more than others saw. His neighbor casting seed on the family field he loved - was not God's passionate love for the land of Israel like that?

Even as he built a village house or a table, his thoughts sometimes turned to another world: was not God building a kingdom for his people?

An inward man, Joseph saw beyond the fields and mountains of the small town of Nazareth, but he said little about his inmost dreams to others.

A quiet man, he kept his own counsel.

Someone someday, perhaps, would understand.

Nor would he say much of something else that made him proud: his descent from King David.

His family could trace its ancestry through generations back to the Shepherd King of Bethlehem, one of Israel's great heroes. By Joseph's time, David's descendants were many, but Jewish tradition said one day the Messiah would be born from one of David's family. The carpenter could not forget a promise such as that.

Engagement and Problem

It was taken for granted in those days that young people got married, usually when a girl was about fourteen and a young man over twenty-five.

Marriages were arranged by parents. And so the marriage of Joseph and Mary, planned by their parents, came about.

Though unmarried young men and women were strictly separated then, in a small town like Nazareth the two had to meet at times.

On those occasions at the market, on the road, during Jewish feasts, Joseph saw Mary briefly. The young girl's beauty seemed to come from a special depth of spirit. He was attracted, and he looked forward to their marriage.

They were engaged at a formal ceremony before family and friends, which gave Joseph the right to call Mary his wife. Then, as was the custom, Mary returned to her own home to wait about a year for the day when she would go to live with her husband.

The Gospel of Luke tells what took place then: "The angel Gabriel was sent from God to a town of Galilee called Nazareth, to a virgin betrothed to a man named Joseph, of the house of David, and the virgin's name was Mary."

The angel announced that a child would be born to her by the power of God, who would save his people from their sins. Mary consented to the angel's request and conceived the child in her parents' home.

When Joseph learned that Mary was pregnant, according to Matthew's Gospel, he was deeply disturbed, not knowing of the angel's visit.

Jewish law demanded he divorce Mary for infidelity, since she had conceived a child that was not his.

He knew he must follow the law as an upright man, but his high regard for Mary and his own kindness made him decide to divorce her quietly so as not to bring her public disgrace.

"Don't Be Afraid..."

"Such was his intention when, behold, the angel of the Lord appeared to him in a dream and said, 'Joseph, son of David, do not be afraid to take Mary your wife into your home. For it is through the Holy Spirit that this child has been conceived in her. She will bear a son and you are to name him Jesus, because he will save his people from their sins.'"... When Joseph awoke, he did as the angel of the Lord had commanded and took his wife into his home." (Mt 1:20-21, 24)

The dream gave Joseph his life's task: he must care for the child and his mother. But it left so much unexplained. What would the child be like? What would he do? And how precisely was Joseph himself to fulfill his role?

The carpenter of Nazareth could only wait until those questions were answered. God alone unfolds dreams.

Vittore Carpaccio. *Flight into Egypt*
(15-16th Century)

Generations before, God spoke in dreams to another Joseph, the son of Jacob. Sold by his brothers into slavery in Egypt, he became Pharaoh's counselor and then the guardian of the Israelite people in the time of famine.

Following his namesake Joseph, whom God led in unexpected ways, the carpenter of Nazareth resolved to trust in his dreams.

He took Mary into his home.

Joseph, the Quiet Father

The story of Christ's birth in Bethlehem is too well known to tell in full. One might notice, however, that Luke and Matthew tell Joseph's part in the event from different perspectives.

In Luke's account, Joseph and Mary travel to Bethlehem, David's own city because Caesar Augustus, the Roman emperor, decreed that a census be taken throughout the world.

Joseph remains quietly in the background when the child is born and shepherds come to adore.

The couple fulfills Jewish law, arranging for the circumcision of the child and calling him Jesus.

After thirty days, they journey five miles to Jerusalem to present the child to God in the Temple. Old Simeon and Anna praise God for the child they take eagerly into their arms.

Afterwards, Mary and Joseph return with the infant to Nazareth.

Joseph fulfills the usual role of a Jewish father, yet he silently marvels at the signs that accompany Jesus' birth.

Joseph, the Strong Provider

According to Matthew's Gospel, Joseph has a strong role.

Not only does he, as the child's legal father, give Jesus the right to be called a descendant of David, but he protects the child and mother.

Warned in a dream, he takes Jesus and Mary into Egypt to escape from King Herod, who wants to kill the child as a rival to his power.

Like the infant Moses, threatened by Pharaoh's massacre of Jewish infants, the child Jesus must be guarded from wicked forces threatening his life.

Joseph, directed by his dreams, is the watchman to whom God entrusts the son and his mother at a dangerous time.

The young family then returned to their home in Nazareth to live among their relatives and friends.

They said nothing about the child.

God, who provided mysteriously for his birth, would unfold the rest in time.

The prophet Isaiah had said of the Messiah: "A shoot shall sprout from the stump of Jesse." God had placed the growing child, like a tender plant, in their hands.

Companion and Example for Jesus

Jesus, the Son of God, was known throughout his earthly life as "the carpenter's son," the son of Joseph. Growing up as children do, he would naturally acquire some of Joseph's traits, perhaps his walk or some of his expressions of speech.

From Joseph, Jesus first learned about the people of the village, their sorrows and their joys. Nor could Joseph's love for Mary and his love for people be mistaken by the young child.

From Joseph, Jesus learned how to use a carpenter's tools and after awhile he worked at his side. The rabbis said: A father who does not teach his son a trade teaches him to steal. Jesus learned to work hard and steadily at the carpenter's trade.

The two were constant companions at the synagogue in Nazareth. Together they celebrated regularly the great Jewish feasts, listened to the scriptures, and journeyed as pilgrims to Jerusalem.

More than anything else, Jesus saw in Joseph a simple, holy man who trusted God with all his heart. Someone like Joseph, so unassuming, so steady, so quietly attentive to God, was like a treasure hidden in a field. He could easily go unrecognized.

But it would not be so.

Bartolome Esteban Murillo. *The Holy Family with the Little Sparrow* (17th Century)

G. B. Galli. *The Older Joseph and the Child*
(16th Century)

Later, when Jesus began to teach, can we not hear in his parables and lessons memories of Nazareth and the simple wisdom of Joseph the carpenter?

An old tradition says that Joseph died when Jesus was nineteen. Most likely his family was with him when he made that dark journey. Tradition rightly says he died a happy death.

And how could it be otherwise?

For he served God without question, doing God's work until the end, and Jesus and Mary were at his side.

WHAT DOES TRADITION SAY ABOUT JOSEPH?

Devotion to St. Joseph developed slowly in the church.

Early Christian stories originating in Syria and Egypt from the year 150 onward depict him as an old man, a widower, who marries the Virgin Mary and faithfully cares for her and the child.

The image of an aged Joseph usually appears in medieval art, drama and poetry. It is the common image of Joseph in the Eastern churches.

The image arose because an aged Joseph would more likely ensure the perpetual virginity of Mary. And if he were a widower, the brothers of Jesus mentioned in the gospels (Mt 12:46) might refer to Joseph's children by a previous marriage.

Scholars today generally dismiss these characterizations. Joseph was most likely a young man, not previously married.

Venerable Bede (+735) summed up early Christian thought about Joseph's role: "It was necessary that Blessed Mary have a husband who would vouch for her reputation and care faithfully for our Lord and Savior. Joseph offered the child in the Temple as the law prescribed. He brought him and his mother into Egypt to avoid danger and brought them back from there. He did everything needed for a child so vulnerable and so small."

Recognition: Fifteenth Century

Until the fifteenth century, however, Joseph received little recognition, remaining as the gospels often present him, in the background.

In the fifteenth and sixteenth centuries, theologians, preachers, spiritual writers and saints of the Western church turned their 41 attention to Joseph. Lives of the saint, written then, present him as devoted young husband and father, an example for workers, a patron for the dying, and a protector for the church during the crisis of the Reformation.

St. Teresa of Avila (+1582) and other important spiritual figures of those times praised the saint's interior life. Joseph, who listened to God's voice within his heart, was an example to Christians who, confused by their own times, turned for guidance to prayer and an interior life.

Teresa ascribed her cure from sickness when she was twenty-six years old to his intercession. Her popular writings were an important stimulus to Catholic devotion to Joseph.

"I can never remember asking him for anything and not being answered," Teresa wrote.

Catholics setting out for the New World of the Americas placed new towns and churches under the patronage of Joseph who watched over Jesus and Mary in the faraway land of Egypt.

Numerous places and churches in South America and parts of North America settled by the French bear the saint's name.

He is the patron of Mexico, Canada, Belgium and China.

Numerous religious communities, like the Sisters of St. Joseph, founded in LePuy, France, about 1648, called upon the saint's trust in God's providence to guide their ministry in a changing world.

The feast of St. Joseph on March 19 was introduced into the Church's liturgy on 1479.

Francesco De Rossi.
The Holy Family (16th Century)

Pope Pius IX, at the close of the First Vatican Council, proclaimed Joseph the patron of the universal church.

Pope Pius XII established the feast of St. Joseph the Worker (May 1) in 1955 to emphasize the dignity of the Christian worker.

John the Baptist

Six months before the birth of Jesus Christ, God sent John the Baptist, the last great prophet to Israel, to prepare for the coming of his Son.

He was born, as Luke's Gospel reports, "in a town of Judah, in the hill country" a short distance from Jerusalem. John's father, Zachary, belonged to a Jewish priestly family whose members served in the Temple for two-week periods during the year. Elizabeth, his mother, was a relative of Mary, the mother of Jesus.

They were good-living people, but they had no children and were both well along in years.

Zachary's Vision

John's birth took place in a miraculous way. One day, while serving in the Temple, Zachary was chosen by lot to enter the holy place during evening prayer to offer incense to God.

Suddenly, the angel Gabriel appeared and told him, "Do not be afraid, Zachary, your prayer has been heard. Your wife Elizabeth is to bear a son, and you are to name him John. You will have joy and many will rejoice at his birth, for he is to be great in the sight of the Lord...He will go before the Lord with the Spirit and power of Elijah and turn the hearts of parents to their children, and the rebellious to the ways of wisdom."

At first, Zachary refused to believe the angel's words because he and his wife were too old to have a child.

For not believing, he lost his voice and remained speechless until his child was born nine months later, as the angel promised.

Then, when family and friends asked what the infant's name should be, Zachary took a writing tablet and wrote: "John is his name."

We know almost nothing about John's early life except that, breaking family tradition, he did not follow his father as a priest serving in the Temple.

Sometime in his youth, perhaps because his parents may have died, he went to live in the wilderness near the Dead Sea, about a day's journey from his home.

There God prepared him for his great mission.

The Judean Wilderness

The Judean Wilderness, a sacred place to the Jews, bordered on the vast Arabian desert to the east. Centuries before John's arrival there, the tribes of Israel had journeyed through this desert from Egypt in search of the Promised Land.

They were tired from the long march that had taken so many years. Yet Moses led them on, over the hard terrain where water was scarce and trees and plants were few. Only

George Angelini. *John Baptizing Jesus in the River Jordan (Contemporary)*

The mountains near the Qumran community. The Dead Sea Scrolls were found in the caves of these mountain,

faith in God sustained them.

As they neared the Dead Sea, the old leader climbed the heights of Mount Nebo where he saw the land God had promised in the distance across the Jordan River.

Moses died on the mountainside, but before his death he urged his people to cross the river and complete their journey.

Ever afterwards, Jews came to the Judean wilderness seeking to recapture the ancient faith of their forebears. They found desert air purer and saw life more simply living on the hard, memorable land that seemed to belong to God alone.

The Qumran Community

Some who came to the Judean wilderness formed communities like the one recently discovered by archeologists at Qumran near the Dead Sea.

Strongly religious people, these inhabitants of the desert rejected what they saw as the compromise and spiritual lukewarmness of mainstream Judaism. So they lived apart, hoping for a Messiah and Teacher to bring renewal to their nation and end foreign domination.

Outsiders saw them as peaceful people who avoided the cities and did not marry.

They lived alone in the caves that pocketed the hill country, but came together for meals and prayer and some common work. Known as expert farmers, herdsmen, beekeepers, and craftsmen, they provided for their own few needs from the sparse resources of the desert.

With remarkable ingenuity they worked the few patches of fertile land that existed around the Dead Sea and created an irrigation system that made the desert bloom.

Their main interest, however, was studying and copying the sacred writings of their Jewish tradition. Day and night, these religious people studied, prayed and pondered over God's word.

The Promised Land across the Jordan still waited for a faithful people, they believed, and when the day of the Lord came they would be the ones to inhabit it.

Isaiah the prophet said that God would announce that day "in the desert."

John may have lived in a settlement like Qumran for awhile and learned many of their ways. Eventually, however, he left them to begin a mission of his own.

A Place for Revolution

Besides people like those at Qumran, Jewish revolutionaries also inhabited the Judean wilderness.

In 6 A.D., after the failure of a bloody revolt led by Judas the Galilean against the Romans and their puppet rulers, bands of his followers escaped to wage a guerrilla campaign for Jewish independence from these barren hills.

Disturbed by the occasional raids of these fierce fighters, the Roman authorities and their local allies kept a wary eye on anyone coming from the desert.

Called to the Jordan

The word of the Lord came to John the son of Zachariah in the wilderness and he went into all the region about the Jordan preaching a baptism for the forgiveness of sins. (Luke 3:2-3)

From the Judean wilderness, John first went a short distance to the lower Jordan valley where the river flows into the Dead Sea. This area, too, was hallowed by heroic events and figures of the Jewish past.

There, coming from the desert after the death of Moses, Joshua had led the Israelites over a river ford - a shallow spot where the river can be waded - and up the road to conquer the city of Jericho and enter the "land flowing with milk and honey."

In the Steps of Elijah

Later, in the eighth century B.C., the great prophet Elijah, who preached reform when Israel was turning to worship the false gods of the wicked Queen Jezebel, began his mission in the lower Jordan valley.

God sent ravens to the Wadi Cerith near the river to feed the prophet during the time of terrible drought that marked the beginning of his preaching.

At the end of his life, after preaching throughout Israel, Elijah returned to the lower Jordan, and crossing the east bank of the river, he disappeared mysteriously on a mountain nearby.

His grieving followers encamped near the spot, begging God to send them a portion of their master's spirit.

Later Jewish tradition said that Elijah would return - most likely to the same river area - to announce the Day of the Lord, God's final coming.

And so when John came dressed in a rough camel hair cloak, like Elijah of old, and preached with great power at this memorable spot, people wondered: "Has Elijah returned?"

Preacher to a Pilgrim People

The place assured John of a large audience because it was on a major road to Jerusalem.

Historic Sea of Galilee, Israel. The meandering Jordan River joins the Sea of Galilee at the northern tip of the lake, exits at its southern extremity, and flows through the Jordan Valley to the Dead Sea. Pictured here is the tranquil spot where the river enters the Sea of Galilee.

Crowds of pilgrims, especially from Galilee, stopped to rest there on the river bank before journeying up to the Holy City to celebrate their great feasts.

John's hearers, then, were not simply merchants on their way to market or travelers off to visit their families.

They were pilgrims whose hearts were set to hear the word of God. They came from every walk of life. Even tax collectors and mercenary soldiers - occupations looked down upon by religious Jews - were among them.

The man they heard was bound to impress them.

John's Message

"Prepare the way of the Lord. Reform your lives," John told them.

"The kingdom of heaven is at hand ... The day God will judge you has come. You stand before him even now. You are not only answerable to yourselves, or to your family, or to some people. You must give an account before God for your life. And it's not enough to count on your descent from Abraham or your Jewish blood. You must speak for yourself before God."

John's message was a practical one.

"Anyone who has two coats should give one to someone who has none. And if you have more food than you need, do the same thing.

"Tax collectors," he said, "collect no more than is due. Do not cheat or steal.

"Soldiers, don't rob or bully anyone. Be content with what you have."

"Who are you?" they asked him. "Are you

47

Elijah? or Moses? or the Messiah?"

"No," John replied. "I am the voice crying out in the desert: 'Prepare the way of the Lord.'"

He led those who responded to his preaching into the water of the Jordan where he poured water on them and they washed themselves clean.

"I baptize you with water. Someone mightier than I am is coming. He will baptize you with the Holy Spirit and fire. I am not worthy to untie his sandals."

His Reputation Spreads

Word that a prophet was preaching at the Jordan spread quickly over the land.

Not only did many come to hear John and be baptized, but some joined him as followers. Among them were some fishermen from Galilee, two brothers - Peter and Andrew - and Philip and Nathaniel. They admired the man for his fierce honesty and ascetical lifestyle. Something from the world beyond set him apart.

John's activity disturbed others, however.

In Jerusalem, the ruling class worried about a preacher from the desert who criticized them for neglecting God's law.

And the Romans and their allies became alert for any sign that the new prophet could be calling for revolution.

The Meeting

On a certain day, Jesus came to the River Jordan and asked John to baptize him.

"I need to be baptized by you," John said, recognizing who Jesus was.

"Let it be so," Jesus insisted, and entering the water, waited in prayer for John to pour water on him.

The heavens suddenly opened and God's voice was heard:

"This is my beloved Son in whom I am well pleased. Listen to him."

From that time on, Jesus began his ministry. The promised Messiah had come.

The next day John pointed Jesus out to two of his followers, one of whom was Andrew, the brother of Simon Peter.

Having met Jesus, Andrew became his disciple.

Then he called Peter.

Philip and Nathaniel soon joined them as companions of Jesus.

His Final Task

One more thing awaited John - persecution and death.

Herod Antipas, a cruel, cunning man who gained his political power by shrewdly courting favors from the Roman Caesars, ruled the region where John preached.

For most of the winter months he lived at a sumptuous palace in nearby Jericho, enjoying the warm climate of the Jordan valley.

His spies, who were everywhere, kept him constantly informed about John and the excitement his preaching caused among the people. Their reports caused Herod to fear.

And the ruler had reason to be afraid.

At the time John began his ministry, Herod had fallen in love with his niece Herodias, the wife of his half-brother, and so he decided to divorce his wife, the daughter of King Aretus, who ruled the neighboring Nabateans.

Fearing for her own life, Herod's wife fled back to her own land and relations between the two rulers rose to an explosive level that led, years later, to war between the two kingdoms.

on him.

John's preaching aggravated the situation. Like Elijah, he was not afraid of confronting kings.

"It is not your right to take your brother's wife," the Baptist warned.

His hearers, most of them Herod's subjects who despised the overbearing ruler, agreed with the condemnation.

Herod moved quickly to silence the prophet dressed in camel hair. He imprisoned John in the dungeon of his fortress at Machaerus on the eastern side of the Dead Sea. But the prophet's silence was as strong an indictment as his words.

Revenge Claims a Victim

Herodias, a jealous, vengeful woman, was infuriated by the Jewish preacher's condemnation.

When Herod's birthday came, a great banquet was held in the castle and his influential friends, officers and the leading figures of Galilee were there.

At one point, Herodias' daughter, Salome, came in and danced for the delighted guests.

Pleased beyond reason, Herod told the girl: "Ask me for anything you want and I will give it to you."

"What shall I ask for?" the girl whispered to her mother.

"Ask for the head of John the Baptist," came the answer.

When the girl told Herod she wanted John's head on a platter, the king sadly regretted his promise. But, not wanting to appear before his guests as a man who did not keep his word, he granted Salome's request.

His executioner quickly went down to the prison cell and cut off John's head with his sword.

He returned with the head on a platter and gave it to the girl who gave it to her mother.

Afterwards John's disciples came and took his body and buried it and then went off to tell Jesus.

No One Greater Than John

If John had an opportunity during his imprisonment at Machaerus to walk along the castle roof, he could look below at the strange, still water of the Dead Sea - to Jews a sign of God's judgment.

Across the sea, the desert land where God had prepared him for his mission stretched out along the horizon.

Perhaps he could see there some signs of the place where the people of the Qumran community quietly waited for God's visitation.

Beyond the desert were the mountains of Judea and Jerusalem where his father Zachary has served as a priest in the Temple.

And northwards, in the distance, lay the twisting green strip of land that was the Jordan valley, where he had preached and baptized and where his followers anxiously awaited news about his fate.

From birth until death, John had been singled out by God for a unique mission - to prepare the way for the promised Messiah. He was forever faithful to that mission. As it came to end, a more powerful voice than his began to speak in the land.

Jesus always held John's memory dear, and after his death gave him an unsurpassed tribute: "There is no one born of woman greater than John."

So John the Baptist is one of the greatest of the saints who knew Jesus.

En Kerem, a village in the gently rolling hills outside Jerusalem where tradition says John the Baptist was born. In the center is a church dedicated to the prophet and saint.

WHAT THE NEW TESTAMENT SAYS ABOUT JOHN THE BAPTIST

Evidence of Christian devotion to John the Baptist first appears in the gospels and other early Christian writings, though in each of these sources John is seen in a different light.

The Gospel of Mark

In the opening sentences of Mark's narrative, John is described as a messenger, like the prophet Elijah, sent to prepare for the coming of Jesus. John served Jesus as his humble servant; his baptism with water will be completed by Jesus' baptism with the Holy Spirit (Mk 1:2-8).

Mark indicates that John and his followers were active in ministry at the same time as Jesus and his followers, but differences between them, such as their practices of fasting, gradually appeared and distinguished them (Mk 2:18-19).

Mark's Gospel also gives a vivid account of John's death at the hands of Herod and Herodias. The evangelist shows that, like Elijah, the Baptist suffered for confronting the ruling powers of his day, and his death foretold the death of Christ.

In the spirit of his Gospel, Mark holds John up to his readers as a model for those who suffer persecution for justice's sake.

The Gospel of Matthew

Matthew's account of John, though somewhat like Mark's, emphasizes more strongly the hostility of Herod and the Pharisees toward the prophet. Both Jesus and John suffer from people hostile to those whom God sends (Mt 13:57-14:12).

Matthew links John's teaching to the teaching of Jesus so closely that they seem to speak with one voice. They resemble each other, too, in their death.

The Gospel of Luke

Only Luke describes the birth of John, and places it parallel to the birth of Jesus (Lk 1-2). Luke's Gospel sees John as initiating a new period of history when he announces the coming of Christ.

In his infancy stories, the evangelist carefully shows the superiority of Jesus to John, while at the same time an angel indicates the privileged role John plays as precursor of the Messiah. Only Luke mentions that John and Jesus are related.

The Acts of the Apostles reports that John's followers continued to work independently of Jesus' followers even after Pentecost and that the early church sought to convert John's disciples to its own belief (Acts 19:5-6).

The Gospel of John

The fourth Gospel emphasizes the differences between John the Baptist who is only "a voice" and Jesus who is the eternal Word of God. The evangelist subtly presents John as a witness to One far greater than himself. Pointing to Jesus as "the Lamb of God," he directs his own followers to the Messiah, while renouncing any claims to a greatness of his own (John 1).

Some scholars see in the fourth Gospel's presentations of John an attempt by the early church to convert the disciples of John who had not yet embraced the Christian way.

John in the Apocryphal Writings

Mid-second-century Christian stories, imaginatively expanding on the scriptures, circulated other information about John among Christians of the East who wondered about his childhood, as they did about the childhood of Jesus.

"The Gospel of James"

"The Gospel of James" (c. 150 A.D.) relates that when Herod ordered the massacre of little children in the vicinity of Bethlehem after Jesus' birth:

> Elizabeth went up into the hills looking for a place to hide her children, but there was none. So she cried aloud and said, "O mountain of God, receive me, a mother with my child," for she could go on no longer.
> And immediately the mountain opened and received her. And within the mountain a light shone for her. An angel of the Lord was there to protect them.

Guiliano Bugiardi. *John in the Desert (16th Century)*

Herod, the story continues, went in search of Zachary, John's father, and killed him in the Temple. But Elizabeth and her child remained safe.

Pilgrims through the centuries have honored a shrine to John the Baptist inspired by this story at En Kerem in Palestine.

A Fifth-Century "Life of John"

According to the legendary "Life of John" by Serapion, originating in Egypt, while Jesus, Mary and Joseph were at Bethlehem, John and his mother Elizabeth wandered in the desert for five years. Then Elizabeth died.

The Lord Jesus, whose eyes see heaven and earth saw his little cousin John sitting and weeping near his mother, and he began to weep.

When Mary asked him why he wept, Jesus said: "Your cousin Elizabeth has left my beloved John an orphan. He is weeping over her body lying in the mountain."

And Mary began to cry. But Jesus told her "Do not weep, mother, you will see her this very hour."

And mounting a cloud they flew to the wilderness of En Kerem to the spot where John was sitting by the body of Elizabeth.

"Do not be afraid, John. I am Jesus your cousin. I came with my beloved mother to bury your good mother Elizabeth."

And they embraced John.

After they washed her body at the spring of clear water, they buried her. And Jesus and Mary stayed with John for seven days and taught him how to live in the desert.

Seven days later Jesus told his mother: "We must go to the place where my work will begin." But Mary wept over the young

child and urged that he be taken with them.

"This is not my heavenly Father's will," Jesus said. "He must remain in the wilderness till the day when he is revealed to Israel.

"Instead of a desert filled with wild beasts, he will walk in a desert full of angels and prophets. I give him the angel Gabriel as his protector. Do not weep over this child. I shall not forget him."

And behold clouds lifted them up and brought them to Nazareth.

A Model for Monks

From the earliest times, some fervent Christians looked to the life of John the Baptist as a model for their own lives. After all, Jesus had praised him, and many of Christ's own teachings seemed to recommend the style of life John led.

"If you will be perfect, go and sell what you have, give to the poor, and come follow me," Jesus said.

John's simple manner of life followed that teaching.

Some of his followers, like John, would not marry, Jesus said, so that they could promote the kingdom of heaven (Mt 19:12). Their constant attention to prayer and the divine word would enable them to hear God's message and proclaim it in their time.

By the mid-third century, the monastic movement attracted Christian men and women in Egypt and other areas of the Middle East to leave their homes and cities for remote areas where they could live their Christian lives more intently.

Living alone as hermits or gathering with other Christians in communities, they drew upon John's life for inspiration. Some, like John, became great preachers and spiritual leaders in the church. Others, confronting political, social and religious injustice, suffered persecution.

The Lasting Example of John

While John was especially revered by Christians who embraced monasticism, he has been an important figure for all Christians.

Churches and shrines in his honor multiplied after Christianity was granted tolerance by Constantine in the fourth century.

From the earliest times the Western church has celebrated feasts in honor of his birth (June 24) and his death (Aug. 29).

Because he baptized Jesus in the River Jordan, John had always been associated with the Sacrament of Baptism. Baptisteries - that part of the church where baptisms are administered - usually have an image or another reminder of the Baptist who led Jesus to the waters of the Jordan.

Through the centuries he has been a reminder to Christians that asceticism, contemplation and missionary activity must be part of every Christian's life.

The River Jordan. "And in those days Jesus came from Nazareth of Galilee, and was baptized by John in the Jordan." (Mark 1:9)

Peter

Capernaum by the Lake

The town of Capernaum - where so much of Jesus' ministry took place and where Peter and some of his other disciples lived - was situated on the edge of the Plain of Gennesaret on the northwest shore of the Sea of Galilee, an area regarded by many people then as almost a paradise.

"In one sweeping gesture nature gathered every plant and season in this spot," the early Jewish historian Josephus wrote. "People can grow anything here. The temperate climate favors every kind of plant. Walnut trees that like cold grow beside palm trees that thrive in heat, and figs and olives that like a milder climate."

Like the fertile plain, the fresh waters of the lake, eight miles wide and thirteen miles long, were rich, too, in all kinds of fish. Year round, fishermen spent long but profitable hours casting their nets into the blue water. The lake provided a good living despite an occasional storm or a day when they caught nothing. Returning to shore, they sorted out the best fish, preserved them, and shipped them at a comfortable profit to nearby towns and even distant cities throughout the Roman Empire. Fish from the Lake of Galilee, whether fresh, dried, pickled or roasted, was a favorite dish for any table.

Trade Route and Customs Center

Fishing and farming were not Capernaum's only occupations. It was also a customs town, just three miles from the border that separated the territory ruled by Herod Antipas from that of his brother Philip.

A major imperial road passed by the edge of the town, and travelers and merchants from faraway cities like Damascus in Syria had to stop at Capernaum to pay a tax.

A detachment of Roman soldiers was stationed at Capernaum to police that part of the road. And, of course, tax collectors lived there, too.

A Cosmopolitan Town

Living where they did, the Jews of Capernaum were far more involved with their gentile neighbors than were the strict-living Jews of Nazareth, who preferred to live apart in the remote hill country of Galilee. In fact, the relations of these Jews of Capernaum with some gentiles were quite cordial.

Just thirty yards from the house where Peter lived, a new synagogue had been constructed for the town, as a gift from the commander of the local Roman garrison, who genuinely liked the people there. And they liked him.

George Angelini. *Jesus in Peter's boat on the Lake of Galilee (Contemporary)*

Capernaum residents even tried to get along with the tax collectors in town. True, tax collectors could be untrustworthy, yet, how could you trade fish or farm produce without them? They would not be ignored.

Fishermen Family and Associates

Peter, named Simon at birth, originally came from the tiny fishing village of Bethsaida, located further up the coast of the Sea of Galilee. Perhaps drawn by the better fishing grounds around Capernaum and its commercial advantages, his family moved

there when Peter was young.

His father, Jonas, was a fisherman, and Peter and his brother Andrew became fishermen, too.

Another family was a partner in their fishing: Zebedee and his sons, James and John. The two families' business was so good, in fact, that they needed some hired hands to help them with their boats.

Simon married as a young man and, with his wife and mother-in-law, lived in a set of family houses grouped together in a walled compound near the lake. Some say his wife

Fishermen on the Sea of Galilee, near Bethsaida, the home of Peter, Andrew and Philip.

died not long after they were married. If she did, and whether the couple had any children, is not known.

For all their hard work, Simon and his friends were faithful Jews, who kept the Sabbath and the Jewish law and made yearly pilgrimages to Jerusalem for the solemn feasts. On one of those pilgrimages, a dramatic meeting occurred that changed their lives.

Andrew Informs Peter

Going up to Jerusalem for the celebration of a feast, Simon's brother Andrew stopped where the road crossed the Jordan River to hear John the Baptist preaching. Moved by John's words and convinced he was a prophet, Andrew decided to stay on with him

as a disciple. John introduced Andrew to Jesus.

"We have found the Messiah. Come and meet him," Andrew reported to Simon excitedly.

At once Simon went to meet Jesus near the Jordan River. Jesus said to Simon what he said to Andrew, "Come, follow me."

From that time onward, Simon was his chosen companion.

Jesus Makes Simon's House His Home

When Jesus journeyed back north to Galilee, the two brothers accompanied him, joined by two others - Philip and Nathaniel. Eventually, twelve disciples would follow him.

They went first to Cana in Galilee, and at a wedding Jesus turned water into wine. Then they returned to Capernaum on the shore of the lake.

Simon's house in Capernaum was Jesus' home during much of his public ministry. Undoubtedly, Jesus loved it there. One of his first miracles was worked in the little cluster of houses where Peter's family lived. He cured Simon's mother-in-law of a high fever by his touch.

From then on, Simon's house became a place where people came whenever Jesus was there. Not only from the town itself but from places all along the lake and from the towns beyond, the blind, the deaf, the lame and paralyzed flocked to that house and they were made well. Soon, Capernaum was known throughout the land for something more than its climate and the abundance of crops: Jesus Christ was there.

For many reasons, Simon's house and the town itself made an almost ideal setting for the beginnings of Jesus' ministry.

Capernaum was far from Jerusalem, where new religious figures were treated suspiciously by the religious establishment. And unlike Nazareth, intolerant of the outside world, it was a place where new things could be said and done.

Besides, the Roman commander of the local garrison and the ruler of the local synagogue were friendly to Jesus. And even if Herod Antipas, the ruler of Galilee, nervously eyed the new prophet from his nearby capital city of Tiberias, the border of another territory was only three miles away.

For awhile, as increasing numbers of people came to see and hear the new prophet, Simon, Andrew and their friends continued fishing as they had always done, for habits of a lifetime don't easily change. This was especially true of Simon, a person of set ways and convictions. Even more than the other men of Capernaum, he was a man steeped in custom, a practical man concerned for his business and his family. But then one day his settled life was changed.

Simon's Change of Career

Early one morning, returning with no fish after fishing all night, Peter and Andrew saw Jesus talking to a crowd of people by the shore. Turning to Simon who was just beaching his boat, Jesus told him to take his boat out and fish again.

"We have fished all night and caught nothing," Simon told him, "but we will do what you say."

Sailing out onto the sea, they let down their nets, which had hardly touched the water when they were filled to the breaking point with fish.

The House of Peter in Capernaum.

Quickly returning to shore, Simon fell to his knees before Jesus, saying, "Leave me, Lord, I am a sinful man!"

"Follow me," Jesus told him, "and I will make you a fisher of men."

Then, leaving their boats and their nets, their families and their friends, Simon and the others followed Jesus from that time on.

They set out for other towns and places in Galilee. Enthusiastic crowds met them wherever they went, except for Nazareth and a few other places. Jesus taught, cured the sick and even raised the dead to life. Always, Simon was at his side as a loyal friend, enthusiastic and quick to speak his mind, ready for anything, a natural leader among the disciples themselves.

Not that Simon understood everything. Though he loved his Jewish traditions, he was hardly an expert in religious matters. He was a fisherman who knew the mysterious waters of the sea. Yet their mysteries could not compare with the mysterious dimensions of the person he followed now.

Their relationship only deepened with time. Simon was not just a disciple of Jesus or a witness to the wonders he worked. They

Anthony Van Dyck.
Christ Giving the Keys to Saint Peter (17th Century)

He (Jesus) said to them, "Who do you say that I am?" Simon Peter said in reply, "You are the Messiah, the Son of the living God." Jesus said to him in reply, "Blessed are you, Simon son of Jonah. For flesh and blood has not revealed this to you, but my heavenly Father. And so I say to you, you are Peter, and upon this rock I will build my church, and the gates of the netherworld shall not prevail against it. I will give you the keys to the kingdom of heaven. Whatever you bind on earth shall be bound in heaven and whatever you loose on earth shall be loosed in heaven."

(Matthew 16:15-19)

were friends, bound together by a friendship that seemed incapable of being broken.

A Change of Name

Near the City of Caesarea Philippi, Jesus asked his disciples one day, "Who do people say that I am?"

"You are the Christ, the Son of God," Simon quickly answered.

"Blessed are you, Simon, son of Jonas," Jesus said to him. "You are Peter, and upon this rock I will build my church. I will give you the keys of the kingdom of heaven."

From that time, Simon was called Peter and he would have a special place in the ministry of Jesus, who shared things with him that he shared with no one else. With two other disciples, James and John, he witnessed Jesus shining in glory on the mountain of the Transfiguration.

But it was not only Jesus' glory he would share. For Jesus had his enemies. Not everyone welcomed the activity of the teacher from Galilee and his disciples. The Jewish leaders in Jerusalem and other political leaders, stung by his criticism of them and fearing revolution among the people, began a plot to stop him.

Aware of the danger he faced, Jesus told his disciples: "We are going up to Jerusalem, and the Son of Man will be delivered over to be crucified."

Peter and the other disciples hardly heard his words. In their eyes, following Jesus could only bring them success.

The Prediction and Denial

Journeying to Jerusalem for Passover before he died, Jesus gathered his disciples for a final

Caravaggio. *Saint Peter Denying Christ (16th Century)*

meal. Beginning with Peter, he washed their feet as if he were their servant.

At table, he reminded them of his friendship for them, and gave them bread and wine as his body and blood. Then he predicted they would all desert him in his time of trial.

Peter protested, "Even if everyone betrays you, I will not."

"This night," Jesus said, "before the cock crows, you will deny me three times."

Later that evening, Jesus took Peter, James and John with him into the Garden of Gethsemane to pray. Yet while he prayed and was seized by fear, they slept.

Suddenly, they were awakened by a noisy crowd of soldiers who arrested Jesus and dragged him away for trial before the Jewish leaders and Roman authorities.

Peter followed them into the courtyard of the High Priest. Some servants had gathered in one corner of the courtyard around a fire to keep warm in the cold night, and Peter came over to the fire, too.

"Aren't you one of his disciples?" a servant asked him.

"No," Peter replied.

"Are you sure you are not? You speak like a Galilean."

"No, I am not," Peter answered loudly. Then he began to curse and swear that he never knew Jesus.

A rooster suddenly crowed, and Peter 59

remembered Jesus' prediction: three times he would deny him. And Peter went out and wept bitterly.

Transformation

So Peter was not there when Jesus died on Calvary. On Easter Sunday, he was hiding in Jerusalem with the other disciples, ashamed of his cowardice, when some women who were close to Jesus went to anoint his body. They came back with startling news: "He is not there!"

Running to the tomb with John, Peter, too, found the body gone.

Soon that same day, Jesus, risen from the dead, appeared to Peter and then to others. Again and again he returned to reassure them, for they could hardly believe their eyes.

On one of these occasions he said to Peter: "Simon, do you love me?"

"Yes, Lord, you know I love you," Peter answered.

"Feed my lambs and my sheep."

Three times Jesus repeated his question and three times Peter answered, until the words seemed to erase the memory of the previous words of denial. Once again they could walk together as friends.

At Jesus' command, Peter waited in Jerusalem with the other disciples and Mary the mother of Jesus for the coming of the Holy Spirit. When the grace of Pentecost descended on them, their spirits were set on fire and they preached in the Temple and the streets of Jerusalem about Jesus who died and rose from the dead.

Spreading the Word

As great as were the miracles that Jesus performed before his death, they hardly compare to the change the Holy Spirit worked in the disciples at Pentecost.

After Pentecost they saw Jesus in a new way: as God's only Son who had conquered death and brought new life. A new depth of love for him filled their hearts, a new bravery inspired what they said and did. They were no longer frightened and unsure.

Peter spoke as their leader in those early days after Pentecost, and his words were so persuasive that many Jews from all parts of the world who had come to Jerusalem for the feast became believers in Jesus.

The disciple even had the power to heal people. At the gate of the Temple he cured a crippled beggar and crowds gathered enthusiastically around him as they had gathered before around Jesus.

Once more, as they had some months before, the authorities in Jerusalem intervened by trying to crush this movement from Galilee. But nothing, not even jail or beatings or death threats, could prevent Peter and the others from telling the story of the One they loved and knew by faith as the Son of God.

After preaching for some time in the Holy City where the Christian community was now established, Peter went with John into Samaria, and from there to the coast cities of Joppa and Caesarea. His preaching among the Jews made new converts and he performed more miracles there, healing a paralyzed man and returning a dead woman named Tabitha to life.

A Turning Point in Caesarea

Peter's journey to Caesarea became a turning point for the new Christian movement. In that city, the Roman centurion Cornelius embraced the Christian faith.

Caesarea was the Roman capital of Palestine,

where the Roman procurator resided and a considerable garrison of soldiers was stationed. As a base for the foreign conquerors of their land, it was a city Jews avoided if they could.

A Centurion Sees a Vision

But, like the Roman centurion at Capernaum, Cornelius was a gentile and a Roman who admired the Jews and their ancient faith.

An angel spoke to him in a vision: "Cornelius."

He answered in fear: "What is it?"

"Your prayers and kindness have been heard by God. Now send messengers to Joppa and have them bring one called Simon Peter, who is staying as a guest of a certain Simon, a tanner, whose house is by the sea."

He summoned two of his servants and sent them off to Joppa.

Peter's Vision

While they were on their way, Peter was praying on the roof of the house where he was staying. He, too, had a vision. He saw the heavens opening and a great cloth lowered to the earth. In it were animals and birds of all kinds. A voice came to him: "Get up, Peter, and eat."

As a Jew, Peter kept the kosher laws which forbade eating many kinds of meat. So he replied: "I cannot, Lord, because I have never eaten anything impure."

"What God has declared pure you shall not call impure," the voice answered. And the vision ended.

While he was wondering what the vision meant, Cornelius' messengers arrived, asking him to come to the soldier's house.

Peter Understands

The next day Peter went with them to Caesarea where Cornelius met him at the door of his home with his family and close friends. The soldier fell down at Peter's feet and greeted him as one divine. But Peter made him rise, saying: "Get up, I am only human."

Until then, Peter had preached the gospel only to Jews, and as a traditional Jew, avoided contact with gentiles. Now, he entered Cornelius' house to eat with him.

"You know it is against the law for a Jew to associate with a gentile, or enter his house," he said. "But God has commanded me not to call any person impure. Now I see that God shows no partiality and that every nation is acceptable to him."

After preaching to the people assembled there and seeing them filled with the gifts of the Holy Spirit, Peter baptized them and remained there for some days.

From that time, the apostle accepted non-Jews as fellow believers in Christ, and Cornelius' conversion was seen as a sign that God was calling the gentiles to belief in Christ. Later, when the leaders of the church gathered in Jerusalem to discuss gentile converts, Peter insisted that they not be bound by Jewish observances.

"Why do you want to place on their shoulders a yoke that neither our ancestors nor we have been able to bear?" he asked those who sought rigorous Jewish observances from all Christians.

Yet, despite his stand, the Galilean fisherman was probably always more at home with other Jews who spoke his language and kept the older ways. He simply loved the traditions of his childhood too much to

Rome

Athe

Corinth

The Journey of Peter

disown them or lay them aside.

Separation from Judaism, however, was inevitable. Driven from Jerusalem by persecution, Peter lived for a time among the Jews at Antioch in Syria, where the members of the church were first called "Christians." He was revered there and elsewhere as an eyewitness who had followed Jesus from the

beginning. Those hearing him for the first time, and those listening to him again and again, could never mistake his love and faith for his Master. His words carried the special conviction of one who had seen and heard what he spoke of.

But he never omitted, in telling his story, the painful account of his denial.

Pergamum

Ephesus

Damascus

Caesaria

Joppa

Jerusalem

In those early years, Peter guided these new churches wisely as the Rock Jesus predicted he would be. For Jewish Christians trying to reconcile old traditions with their new belief and for gentiles looking for direction in this new way of life, he was a shepherd who led them with care.

And Finally, Rome

After journeys to Corinth and Asia Minor, Peter finally traveled to Rome itself, the capital of the western world. There his life was to end with a brave profession of faith.

Over a million people lived in the crowded city when Peter, probably an old man, arrived

63

in Rome in the middle of the first century. About 60,000 of them were Jews, most of them living in the section across the Tiber River. Some were merchants, powerfully influential at the imperial court; some were slaves, brought to the city as part of the spoils of war.

The Jews of Rome always maintained close relations with Jerusalem and their homeland, and so travelers passed frequently from one city to the other. Certainly, Jewish Christians were already living in the city by 50 A.D., and they must have invited the apostle to come to the capital city.

Besides Jewish Christians, perhaps Romans from Capernaum or Caesarea who had returned to their own country were there to welcome him.

After his arrival, Peter most likely spoke in the synagogues of the city but his activity in Rome was short-lived. A major tragedy brought it to an end.

In 64 A.D. a terrible fire broke out in Rome near the Jewish quarter. For seven days the city burned until almost all its buildings were destroyed.

Some say Nero, the cruel, half-mad emperor then in power, started the fire himself and watched it from a nearby hill, playing a lyre and singing sad songs all the while. To take the blame away from himself, Nero accused the Christians of starting the fire.

Almost two thousand Christians were arrested and cruelly executed, some given to wild animals to be eaten, some crucified, some smeared with pitch and burned alive as torches near the emperor's gardens by the Vatican hill.

"Where Are You Going, Lord?"

According to tradition, Peter was arrested and imprisoned with the others, but then he was freed from jail unexpectedly.

He decided to flee the city, perhaps fearing that he might deny his Master once again in the pressure of the moment. For it was said that he could never tell the story of his former betrayal without shedding tears.

But as he was leaving the city gate, he saw Jesus entering the city.

"Where are you going, Lord?" Peter asked.

"I am going to Rome to be crucified again," Jesus answered.

"Then I am going too," the disciple said, as Jesus disappeared ahead of him.

Returning to the city, Peter was arrested by the police and brought to Nero's field near the Vatican hill.

The cell in the Mamertime Prison, Rome, where tradition says Peter was imprisoned.

There he was crucified head down to the ground, for, according to some reports, he said he was not worthy to die upright on a cross like his Lord Jesus Christ.

His body was taken and buried in the city, and there it lies under the great church that bears his name to this day.

"Amen, Amen, I say to you (Peter), when you were younger, you used to dress yourself and go where you wanted; but when you grow old, you will stretch out your hands, and someone else will dress you and lead you where you do not want to go." Jesus said this signifying by what kind of death he would glorify God. And when he said this, he said to him, "Follow me."
(John 21:18-19)

Guido Reni.
The Crucifixion of Saint Peter
(16-17th Century)

PETER IN THE NEW TESTAMENT

No one among Jesus' disciples is mentioned in the gospels as often as Peter. He is always first on the list of apostles and is cited more than any other. Yet each gospel offers its own portrayal of him.

Mark's Gospel

In Mark's Gospel, written during a time when Christians were persecuted in Rome (65-70), Peter understands Jesus only by experiencing the mystery of the cross. Not by success and fame does Peter become his convinced disciple, but by sharing his suffering and death.

And so, in Mark's Gospel, directed to Christians being persecuted, Peter is a model for every disciple of Jesus. He followed Jesus even to death. Only by sharing in the mystery of the cross and resurrection - taking up one's own cross - can anyone follow Jesus and become his true disciple.

Mark emphasizes, too, that Peter became Jesus' disciple, not just through human attraction or curiosity. As everyone does, he became a disciple by the grace of God. Jesus called Peter (Mk 1:16-18).

Mark's Gospel relates that Peter witnessed secret revelations of Jesus (Mk 5:37; 9:2,5; 14:33) and was sometimes the spokesman for the rest of the apostles (Mk 10:28) during the days of Christ's ministry. Yet at the same time the evangelist bluntly describes the disciple's slow comprehension and false hopes in those early years. Mark describes fully Peter's shameful denial of Jesus.

Matthew's Gospel

Matthew's Gospel - probably written around 80-90 A.D. at Antioch in Syria - gives a special place to Peter, who resided in that city for some time.

In a church where Christian followers of the "liberal" Paul often contended with Christian followers of the "conservative" Apostle James of Jerusalem, Peter stood as a figure of moderation. He was a bridge-person between those wishing to break completely with Judaism and those wanting an exact adherence to Jewish law.

Matthew, therefore, emphasizes Peter's unique role among the apostles by relating his confession at Caesarea Philippi and his designation by Jesus as the Rock on which he will build his church (Mt 16:13-23).

Luke's Gospel and Acts of the Apostles

Luke's Gospel treats Peter with obvious esteem, even to the point of toning down the story of his denial of Jesus in Mark and Matthew.

In the Acts of the Apostles, Luke presents Peter as the leader and spokesman of the apostles after Pentecost who proclaims with great power the message of the gospel to his own people at Jerusalem. Yet he is still a Jew attached to the Temple and his people; God must lead him by a vision to admit gentiles like Cornelius to the church.

John's Gospel

John's Gospel offers some unique details of the apostle. At the synagogue in Capernaum, when many people abandon Jesus because they find his message hard to take, Peter responds to Jesus' question: "Will you also go away?" with a poignant confession of faith: "Lord, to whom shall we go? You have the words of eternal life. We have come to believe and are convinced you are the Holy One of

God." (Jn 6:68)

John alone narrates the incident of the foot-washing at the Last Supper (Jn 13:1-20) and Peter's reunion with Jesus after the resurrection (Jn 21:15-19).

Letters of Peter

The two letters of Peter found in the New Testament were probably written by disciples of Peter who, using his name for the authority it brought their message, exhorted their fellow Christians to be strong in their faith and Christian lives.

EARLY STORIES ABOUT PETER

Early stories about Peter and the other apostles, attempting to furnish information not found in the New Testament, began to appear around the year 200 A.D. They contain some historical traditions, as well as folklore and fiction.

Probably the most important of them, "The Acts of Peter" (c. 190 A.D.), describes Peter traveling to Rome to oppose Simon the Magician, who captivated the city with his wonderful powers. This writing also relates the story of Peter's retreat from the city during persecution in which he meets Jesus and asks him, "Where are you going?"

EARLY SHRINES OF THE APOSTLE

Capernaum

In 1968, archeological investigations in Capernaum uncovered the house of Peter amid the ruins of the old town. The house, archeologists say, had been converted into a "house church" in the latter part of the first century and used for worship by the Jewish

Saint Peter's Basilica, Rome, built in the 16th century by artists such as Michelangelo and Bramante, is located over the traditional tomb of Saint Peter. It is the center of Vatican City, the home of the popes.

Christians of the town as well as Christian pilgrims from afar.

In the late fifth century, an octagonal church honoring the apostle was built over the house, and it continued to be used until the seventh century, when an Arab invasion left the town abandoned and destroyed.

Rome

The grave of Peter on Vatican hill and that of Paul on the Ostian Way were venerated by Roman Christians from the time of their deaths around the year 65 A.D. Recent archeological investigations have confirmed that the gravesite under St. Peter's Basilica belongs to that early time. 67

The Emperor Constantine built the most splendid church in Rome over the grave of Peter about 329 A.D. and it became an instant attraction for pilgrims from all over the Christian world. This church was replaced by the present Vatican Basilica in the sixteenth century.

Peter and the Papacy

Because of the presence of two apostles, Peter and Paul, and its situation as capital of the empire, the church of Rome held a particularly important place in the Christian world from the beginning.

From earliest times, the bishops of Rome have seen themselves as successors of St. Peter, with the responsibility for leadership of the universal church. They have exercised their office as universal shepherd inspired by the words of Christ to Peter: "You are Peter, and on this rock I will build my church."

Rome, the City of Peter

Devotion to Peter, which flourished among Christians in the Middle Ages, was inspired particularly by pilgrims who traveled to Rome from all over Europe to visit the memorials of the apostles and seek forgiveness for their sins.

In Rome itself, they prayed at the Mamertime Prison where the apostle was believed to have been imprisoned; on Janiculum Hill where he was crucified; at the Vatican Basilica where he was buried; and at the church Domine Quo Vadis where he was called to his martyrdom. These visual reminders of the apostle touched the imagination of the medieval pilgrim and the medieval church.

Christians will always be attracted by him. Scripture and tradition present him as an apostle who, though sometimes impetuous

The ancient Mamertime prison, where tradition says Saint Peter was held, is located under this church in the Roman Forum.

and cowardly, was capable of sublime loyalty and love.

To one so frail and human, Christ gave the "power of the keys," the power to forgive sins. A forgiven sinner himself, Peter is a figure Christians remember when they seek divine mercy.

The medieval monk, St. Anselm, prayed to the apostle:

Let your mercy, merciful God,
through the intercession of your dear
apostle Peter,
quickly free me and forgive me my sins.
St. Peter, prince of the apostles,
by the mercy shown to you and the power
given to you,
loose my chains and heal my wounds.
Free me from the kingdom of sin
and lead me to the blessed kingdom of heaven,
where, rejoicing with you,
I may give thanks and praise to
God forever. Amen.

Ugolini Lorenzetti. *Saint Peter* (14th Century)

Andrew

Andrew, the brother of Peter, was one of the first disciples called by Jesus. His family came originally from the town of Bethsaida on the Lake of Galilee in an area heavily populated by Greek-speaking gentiles. Philip, another of the apostles and a friend of Andrew's, also came from that town.

At some time the two brothers moved to Capernaum which is not far from Bethsaida and they lived there with their families within a compound of homes near the lakeshore close to their fishing boats.

According to John's Gospel, Andrew and John, the son of Zebedee, were the first to meet Jesus. They had gone to be with John the Baptist who was preaching by the Jordan River. The Baptist pointed Jesus out to them and they spent a long afternoon with him.

The next day, convinced that Jesus was someone sent by God, Andrew called to his brother Simon to come and meet him. Then Philip joined them too. They all went with Jesus to Galilee and followed him as his disciples until his fateful journey to Jerusalem.

Andrew is mentioned only a few times during Jesus' public ministry. One occasion was when Jesus multiplied the loaves and the fishes.

It was in the fields near the lakeshore between Capernaum and Herod's newly built city of Tiberias at a place called today Heptapegon. A large crowd had followed Jesus to this remote spot and he taught them. As time passed, Jesus asked Philip, "Where can we buy enough food for these people to eat?"

Philip had no answer since the place was far from any source of food. But Andrew said to Jesus, "There is a boy here who has five barley loaves and two fish; but what are these for so many?"

And Jesus, taking and blessing the loaves and the fish, multiplied them and fed the people, just as Moses had given manna to the Jewish people in the desert.

Andrew is again mentioned with his friend Philip during Jesus' triumphal entry into Jerusalem a few days before his death. Some Greek-speaking gentiles, probably converts to Judaism, asked Philip if they might see Jesus. And Philip called his friend Andrew and they both went to Jesus, who rejoiced that the gentiles were now seeking him even as he faced the threat of death:

"Unless a grain of wheat falls to the ground and dies, it remains just a grain of wheat; but if it dies it bears much fruit." (Jn 12:24)

After the death and resurrection of Jesus,

Simone Martini. *Saint Andrew* (14th Century)

Andrew was one of the disciples who received the Holy Spirit at Pentecost. But the New Testament says nothing of his activity afterwards.

WHAT TRADITION SAYS ABOUT ANDREW

St. Andrew has long been honored as the apostle of Greece, and from that region a rich tradition of stories from as early as the second century report his missionary activity and martyrdom. Since they come from ancient tradition they are hard to fully verify.

The Acts of Andrew recall the apostle's journey through the districts of Pontus and Bythinia (along the Black Sea in what is now Turkey) to the regions of Thrace, Macedonia and Achaia (parts of modern Greece). In all these places, Andrew brought people to believe in Christ by teaching and working miracles.

In the city of Patrae in Achaia, according to these traditional stories, Andrew converted Maximilla, the wife of proconsul Egetes. Fiercely possessive of his wife and having no sympathy for her new faith, the proconsul ordered Andrew imprisoned despite the opposition of the people of the city, who revered the apostle.

Egetes proposed to release the apostle if his wife would renounce her faith, otherwise Andrew would die. Hurrying to the prison, Maximilla told Andrew of her husband's proposal.

"I beg you to hold fast," Andrew said to her, "I urge you to love Jesus and not fail . . . Don't worry about me."

"I have him whom I love. I wait and will rest on him. Seeing you weeping, I see that my words have not been in vain and I know my reward will come to me."

And so the proconsul has Andrew scourged and ordered him crucified, instructing the executioners to make sure he died a lingering death. They brought him to the seashore where they set a cross in the sand.

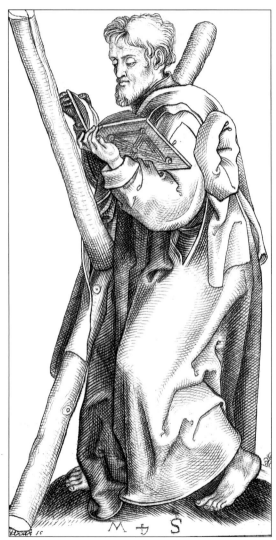

Martin Schongauer. *Saint Andrew with Cross and Holy Scripture* (15th Century)

Andrew spoke to the cross as if it were a thing of mystery:

O cross, rejoice, for a long time you have expected me. I come to you for I know you are mine.

You hold the universe together. One part of you reaches to the heavens, to the heavenly Word. Another part of you reaches right and left to the corners of the earth. And you reach down into the earth to unite to heaven.

O cross, saving instrument of the Most High!

O cross, sign of Christ's victory over his enemies!

O cross, planted in the earth to bear
fruit in heaven!
O cross, may I live through you!

Then they crucified him and Andrew remained on the cross for two days, still speaking words of encouragement to his many disciples who flocked from the city to mourn him. He urged them to be true to their faith in a life so full of deception and passing so quickly away.

Finally he died, and his disciples, Maximilla among them, took his body and buried it with great honor and care.

Later Andrew's remains were brought to Constantinople, and before that city fell to the Turks in 1453, they were taken to Rome. In 1964 Pope Paul VI returned the relics of St. Andrew to the Greek Orthodox church at Patrae in a gesture of reconciliation between the two Christian churches.

St. Andrew is also the patron saint of Scotland. The city of St. Andrew took its name from a sixth-century shrine of the saint.

His feast day is celebrated by the Christian churches of the East and West on November 30.

James, the Son of Zebedee

The Fishing Town

In Jesus' time, the Sea of Galilee was a good provider for the families living along its shores. Year round, except for the Sabbath and the Jewish holidays, fishermen pushed their boats from the rocky beach and rowed or sailed to the rich fishing grounds offshore in search of a catch. Usually they fished through the night and then sold their fish fresh the next day, while preserving a good portion for sale in distant markets.

James and John were the sons of Zebedee, who lived in Capernaum. Probably fishing had been in their blood for generations. James must have been older than John, since he is usually mentioned first in the gospel accounts. They were quick-tempered young men called "sons of thunder" by those who knew them best.

Related to Mary

Their mother's name was Salome, and she was probably the sister of Mary, the mother of Jesus. Later she followed Jesus through Galilee with other women companions and finally stood with Mary beneath his cross on Calvary when he died.

Fishing was a work where people - especially quick-tempered people - had to get along. When the nets were dropped and hauled in, one man depended on another. The boats were small and the hours were many. Far better to have those you knew, your own family or friends, at your side. It was the kind of work that made men into close life-long companions.

James and John, along with their father Zebedee and some hired men, usually fished with Simon and Andrew, two brothers who were their partners and friends. Their families must have lived nearby in Capernaum.

Jesus Takes Up Residence

According to the gospels, Jesus called the two sets of brothers to follow him one morning as they mended their nets after returning from fishing.

By then, Jesus must have been living in Capernaum for some time, most likely at Simon's house. For earlier, Andrew (Simon's brother) and John (the brother of James) had met Jesus beyond the Jordan River where John the Baptist was preaching. They introduced Jesus to Simon. And when John the Baptist was arrested by Herod, they invited Jesus to the safety of their own town of Capernaum.

Soon this group formed the innermost circle of Jesus' companions, and so they saw the startling things he began doing there.

They probably witnessed the cure Jesus worked for Peter's mother-in-law when he first came to Capernaum and the steady stream of people with sicknesses of all kinds who came seeking to be cured. That day the whole town seemed to gather at the door of Peter's house. Some days later when Jesus left to teach in the nearby villages, James and John and Simon and Andrew followed him.

When he returned to Capernaum, as he often did during Jesus' ministry, James, like the others, probably went back to fishing again, taking his place with his father and the hired hands in the family boat. After all, it was the way he made his living.

Excitement

But more and more, like the others, his eyes turned to the land instead of the sea. For he saw that wherever Jesus went a mighty net was cast out and all kinds of people came to him. And Jesus told James, as he told his companions: "Come, and I will make you fishers of men." One of the most dramatic of Jesus' miracles that James witnessed took place in Capernaum itself. The young daughter of Jairus, an officer of the local synagogue, was at the point of death. Her father hurried to Jesus and said: "Come and put hands on her, so that she may live."

Martin Schongauer.
Saint James with Pilgrim Staff
(15th Century)

Yet even as they were leaving for his home, some people came to Jairus with the message: "Your daughter is dead. You don't have to bring the Teacher."

But Jesus reassured him: "Don't be afraid; just have faith."

People were weeping and crying loudly when they came to the house and Jesus said to the mourners: "There's no need to cry. The child is not dead but sleeping."

The people thought he was ridiculous. But he told them to stay outside, and taking Peter, James and John, and the child's father and mother, he entered the room where the child was.

Taking her hands he said to her, "Talitha koum," which means, "Little girl, I tell you arise!"

The girl, who was about twelve years old, got up and began walking around.

They were astounded. Jesus told them to keep this quiet and sent her mother to get the girl something to eat.

Hopes of Glory

Could anyone not be excited by a wonderful thing like this? James thought it was extraordinary. Surely a sign of God's power. Could the wonders worked by Jesus mean that the kingdom promised by God to his people was coming?

Despite the cautions Jesus gave, James' imagination, like that of the other disciples, raced excitedly to what might lie ahead if he followed them.

Was Jesus the Messiah, Son of David? Centuries before God had called the young shepherd David from the quiet pastures of Bethlehem to be a warrior and leader of his people. And David, in a series of brilliant campaigns, conquered almost all of Palestine, established a powerful kingdom, and entrusted high positions in government to his close aids.

Or perhaps, as many people were saying, Jesus was another prophet like the fiery Elijah, who would purify the faith of the Jewish people and stiffen their opposition to foreign domination.

Conjectures like these prompted James and his brother John to ask Jesus on one occasion to give them leading roles in his future kingdom. Indeed, they were his cousins. The other disciples were indignant when they found out about their ambitious maneuvering to gain power.

In response, Jesus told the two brothers they misunderstood the kind of kingdom he was seeking. Gathering his disciples together, he spoke to all of them about the true nature of power: "Whoever wishes to be great among you will be your servant; whoever wishes to be first among you will be the slave of all. For the Son of Man did not come to be served but to serve, and to give his life as a ransom for many."

On another occasion when they were traveling with Jesus to Jerusalem through Samaria, they were refused hospitality at an unfriendly Samaritan village. In anger, James and his brother John said to Jesus: "Lord, do you want us to call down fire from heaven to consume them?" (For the prophet Elijah in his lifetime had called down fire from heaven to punish his enemies.) But Jesus rebuked them and they went to another village.

Missing the Point

Indeed during the ministry of Jesus, James,

like the other disciples, only partially understood the wonders he worked and the words he said. Understanding came slowly to them all. But the most difficult thing for them to understand was what happened to Jesus in his final days.

As they journeyed up to Jerusalem for the Passover feast, Jesus' disciples certainly knew of threats against his life and warnings of danger. He had made enemies as well as friends by what he said and did. Yet from all they had seen they were convinced nothing could harm him, even though he predicted to them his approaching death.

Watching Fear in the Garden

That Thursday night before he died was an unusually emotional one. They ate the Passover meal together and Jesus spoke of giving his body and blood for them and for all the world as he took the bread and the cup of wine and gave it to them to eat and drink.

Afterwards Jesus asked James, as well as Peter and John, his closest companions among the twelve, to accompany him to the garden called Gethsemane on the hill outside the city, where he often went to pray. There he left them to go alone among the olive trees a short distance away. They watched him fall on his knees in distress and begin to cry aloud to God, his Father, for relief.

They had seen nothing like this before. Never before was Jesus so uncontrollably afraid. In the shadows of the night they saw his body driven restlessly by fear and they listened to the cries of his voice. But in time, their eyes grew tired and their spirits heavy, so they wrapped themselves in their heavy cloaks and sought peace in sleep.

Hiding

Unlike his brother John or his mother Salome, who later stood beneath the cross, James abandoned Jesus completely when the soldiers arrested him in the garden that night. He did not even attempt to follow them to the courtyard of the high priest as Peter did. Like most of the twelve, he fled immediately when Jesus was seized and went into hiding while Jesus was put to death.

But after the resurrection of Christ, James was his disciple again and this time he did not fail.

The Cup

Like the others who saw Jesus risen from the dead, he began to understand the kingdom he came to bring. After receiving the Holy Spirit at Pentecost, James too spoke about Jesus to the people of Jerusalem and to the Jews visiting the Holy City from all parts of the world. In the growing Christian church of Jerusalem, James became a prominent figure.

In the year 41, Herod Agrippa, the grandson of Herod the Great, became king of Judea and ruler of the city of Jerusalem. Educated in Rome, he was a favorite of the emperors of that time. He also knew how to please his new subjects, especially the powerful Jewish ruling class that played a key role in his kingdom.

When the Jewish Sanhedrin complained to him about Christians threatening the peace of Jerusalem, Herod sent his soldiers to seize James, the son of Zebedee, and had him executed by the sword. Strike the shepherd, Herod reasoned, and the sheep will scatter.

One early tradition says that as James was being brought to trial, one of the soldiers leading him to court was so moved by his

Gethsemane, the place on the Mount of Olives, facing the city of Jerusalem, where tradition says Jesus prayed and was arrested the night before he died. An ancient olive tree, like those common in Jesus' time, marks the traditional place of Jesus' last agony.

faith that he himself became a Christian and suffered death along with the apostle. As the two made their way to the place of execution, the soldier asked James to pray that he be forgiven his sins.

"Peace be with you," James said, and embraced him.

Years before this, James and his brother John had asked Jesus for a position of power in his kingdom.

"You do not know what you are asking," Jesus replied. "Can you drink the cup I am going to drink?"

"We can," they said to him.

"My cup indeed you will drink," Jesus promised them.

And so the prediction of Jesus came true. James did drink from Jesus' cup. Among the apostles, he was the first to lay down his life for Jesus Christ.

What Later Tradition Says About James

Some Christian writers of the fourth century report that one of the apostles went to Spain.

And a sixth-century story identifies James as the apostle. It relates that he preached in Spain only briefly and converted only a few of the natives before returning to Jerusalem and his death.

Yet relics said to be of St. James were discovered in Compostela in Galicia in northwestern Spain in the ninth century. The discovery was a major event in Spanish history and culture. A shrine in honor of the saint grew in importance as a major pilgrimage center for the people of Spain and Europe, rivaling even Rome and Jerusalem in its popularity.

From the ninth century onward, James was the patron of the Spanish peoples and a rallying symbol for them in their fight to free their land from the Moors. At four battles - Clavijo (9th c.), Simancas (10th c.), Coimbra (11th c.) and Las Navas de Tolasa (1212) - legends say he appeared as a warrior astride a great white horse with a sword in his hand. Throughout the Middle Ages, soldiers and knights especially came as pilgrims to Compostela to seek the saint's protection.

In 1492, when Spain was finally free of Moorish domination, King Ferdinand and Queen Isabella came to Compostela to give thanks to St. James in the name of the Spanish people.

But how ancient are the relics of St. James? Since pilgrims from Galicia were frequent visitors to the Holy Land as early as the fourth century, they may have carried these relics back to their native land.

Colorful legends from medieval times, however, took the story back further to the time of the apostle himself, saying that disciples of James fled with his body after he was beheaded and, escaping by boat, drifted to the coast of Spain where, after many adventures, they buried him.

These legends about James appear frequently in medieval art, and numerous churches in his honor were built in Spain, France, England, and later in the Spanish colonies of the New World. Cities such as Santiago, Chile, and Santiago, Cuba, are named after him.

The feast of St. James is July 25.

John, the Son of Zebedee

From childhood, John, "the disciple whom Jesus loved," lived in Capernaum. His father Zebedee was a fisherman; his mother Salome was probably a sister of Mary the mother of Jesus. When they were old enough, John and his brother James followed their father to his boat on the Sea of Galilee. Later they left everything to follow Jesus.

Even as a young boy, John absorbed the passion for religion found in the Jewish people of his town. Every Saturday morning the men, women and children of Capernaum gathered in early daylight in their handsome synagogue to sit on benches along the walls or on the stone floor, facing the wall toward Jerusalem.

There the seven-branch candle stick burned near the reading desk as the morning light began to stream from behind it through the windows in the wall. The leader of prayer stood and raised his voice to praise God who had a covenant with his people through Abraham, Isaac and Jacob. And the people responded loudly, "Amen."

Then the Ark, a wooden chest containing the scrolls on which were written the first five books of scripture, the Torah, was brought forth. One of the scrolls was unfolded and read in the morning light, first in Hebrew and then in Aramaic, the everyday language of Palestine. When the reading was finished, the scroll was replaced in the Ark and another blessing proclaimed.

A speaker, perhaps an official of the synagogue, a member of the community or a visitor, gave a sermon on the reading from the Law. Besides recalling the great works of God found there, he would remind them to be faithful to the smallest laws and customs of everyday Jewish life.

The service was completed by a reading from the prophets and some prayers. Then people left the synagogue to celebrate the rest of the Sabbath day. The experience was like a spiritual bread nourishing their hearts.

A Passion for Religion

John, like any Jewish boy of his time, under a teacher began studying the Torah at the synagogue with other young boys around the age of five. For half a day, six days a week for the next five years, he would learn the words of the Law phrase by phrase until he knew it almost by heart. "In the beginning God created the heavens and the earth . . . ." Later, for another few years he would study the Talmud, the oral law, under the direction of a teacher. This kind of education kept Judaism strong for generations.

George Angelini. *John in the Empty Tomb on Easter Morning (Contemporary)*

Segna di Buonaventura. *Saint John the Evangelist* (14th Century)

Wall of the temple in Jerusalem. Only the lower rows of stone are from the original temple. Some of them weighed thirty tons. After the Jewish uprising in 67 A. D., Roman legions razed the temple stone by stone.

John's passion for his religious tradition, however, went far beyond his companions' and grew stronger through the years.

Reflective by nature, he loved thinking about God's way with the world and its people. Faith captivated his imagination and enlarged his soul. Somehow, he believed, manna still fell from heaven and water still flowed from a rock as in the days of Moses. One just had to look for it.

Priest in the Family

"Three times a year all your men shall appear before the Lord your God." So had Moses commanded in the law.

From his earliest years John must have joined the thousands of Jewish pilgrims who flocked to Jerusalem and the Temple of God for the great feasts of Passover, Tabernacles and Weeks. He found lodging in the city more easily than most pilgrims, for John's family was related to a priestly family serving in the Temple and was known even to the high priest.

In fact, Jerusalem, its Temple and its feasts were particularly dear to John. The ancient rites and institutions were sacred to him. Though quarreling factions of Sadducees and Pharisees, priests and royal officials, made Jerusalem a place of continual intrigue and unrest, the city still pointed to a world yet to come. Despite everything the Holy City shone with a divine light.

Drawn to John the Baptist

On one of his Jerusalem pilgrimages as a young man, John, with Andrew the brother of Simon Peter, met John the Baptist who was 83 preaching near the Jordan River, and they became his disciples.

The sons of Zebedee the fisherman and the son of Zachary the priest were probably relatives, but they were not drawn together simply by ties of flesh and blood. The Baptist's words and way of life moved John deeply when they met. It was as if God's word were now suddenly alive in a holy man. The fiery preacher spoke of something great that was soon to happen. So John and Andrew stayed on with him in the dry lands beyond the Jordan.

There they met Jesus when John pointed him out to them, and they followed him back to Galilee to their own town of Capernaum.

The Disciple Jesus Loved

Each of his disciples remembered Jesus in a particular way, and so John's memories were distinctly his own. One memory he treasured above all: he was "the disciple whom Jesus loved."

From the time they met in the Jordan valley, John became one of Jesus' trusted friends. Along with his brother, James, and Simon Peter, John was at Jesus' side through most important events of his ministry. True, family ties bound them together - Jesus and John were probably cousins - but like his bond with the Baptist, John's relationship to Jesus came from a deeper source.

It may have been the reflective nature they shared. Of all Jesus' disciples, John was most likely to understand him. Not everything, to be sure. But John, listening and seeing the wonders Jesus did, saw a hint of something beyond, which could hardly be put into words. As they visited the synagogues of Galilee and

went as pilgrims to Jerusalem for the various feasts, the ancient texts and rites seemed to welcome the prophet as if they had been expecting him for years. In Jesus John saw God's word become flesh. And he wondered what it all meant.

The gospels, however, reveal another side of John's character that Jesus knew too. The apostle and his brother, James, are described as "sons of thunder." Though reflective and deeply religious, John was also capable of sudden anger and bold ambition. Yet these faults did not prevent Jesus from loving him.

The Memories Only John Tells

Through John we know the stories of the wedding at Cana in Galilee, the Samaritan woman who met Jesus at the well, the cure of the man born blind, the raising of Lazarus from the dead, and other incidents not mentioned in the synoptic gospels. He remembered too so many of the words and teachings of Jesus that were spoken in the synagogues and in the Temple area at Jerusalem. And he could recall the growing conflict that arose between Jesus and many of the Jewish leaders.

When Jesus went up to Jerusalem with his disciples to celebrate Passover for the last time, it was John and Peter who made arrangements for the room where they were to eat their sacred supper. The memories of that night and the days that followed became fixed in the disciple's mind.

Before supper, Jesus took off his outer garment and, kneeling before his twelve disciples, washed their feet. "Love one another as I have loved you," he told them.

John was at Jesus' side in the supper room when he announced sadly to them: "One of

The traditional site of the Last Supper, located on Mount Zion in Jerusalem .

you is about to betray me." Leaning over to Jesus, the disciple asked him who it was. When Judas was pointed out, John watched the traitor leave and go out into the night.

He could not forget what Jesus said and did that night.

At the Scene on Calvary

When Jesus was arrested in the garden, John and Peter followed the crowd to the house of Annas, who was father-in-law of Caiaphas the high priest. Since John was known to the people there he was allowed to enter the courtyard. In turn, he spoke to the gatekeeper who allowed Peter to come in.

He heard them questioning Jesus and listened to his response. As the night hours passed, the disciple saw no sign that his friend would be released. Rather, as they led Jesus to

Caiaphas and then in the morning to Pilate, John realized that the worst had happened: it was now likely that Jesus would be sentenced to death.

Hurrying through the streets of the city, which was crowded with pilgrims who had come up for the feast, John must have brought the tragic news to Mary, the mother of Jesus, who had come from Galilee with John's mother, Salome, and the other women following Jesus. As news of the death sentence came from Pilate that day, they quickly went to the place of execution outside the city gate - Calvary.

There they stood and saw him crucified.

They watched as the soldiers pushed Jesus along to the place, and they saw him stripped of his clothes and nailed to the cross. They drew as close to him as they could, so as to hear any words he would say.

The Last Supper (detail).
14th Century.

85

When Jesus saw his mother and the disciple there whom he loved, he said to his mother, "Woman, behold, your son." Then he said to the disciple, "Behold, your mother." And from that hour he took her as his own.

The Water and the Blood

He looked on as Jesus died. With his death every sign of hope seemed gone. Yet even as he watched the grim ritual of crucifixion, John saw something the soldiers did which he later recognized as a sign from God after all.

Since the Passover feast, a joyful day recalling God's deliverance of his people, was about to begin, the Jewish leaders asked Pilate to make sure that Jesus and the thieves crucified with him were indeed dead and their bodies removed as quickly as possible so that the feast day would not be disgraced by the sight of death.

So the soldiers did as Pilate ordered. One of them thrust his lance into Jesus' side, although he was already dead, and immediately blood and water flowed out. In this apparently insignificant incident, remembered later, John saw an ironic sign from God.

Indeed, Jesus' death was for the deliverance of his people. The Paschal lamb was just a sign of Jesus the Lamb of God, and the blood and water that flowed from his side, far from bringing disgrace, brought life to the land.

Only in time, however, did John understand these things. As he mourned Jesus' death, carried his body to the tomb for burial and attended to Mary, the mother of Jesus, he saw little meaning in it all.

With Peter at the Tomb

86 On Easter morning when the women who

Martin Schongauer. *The Burial of Jesus* (15th Century)

went to the tomb to finish anointing the body of Jesus returned with the astonishing news that he was not there, John ran with Peter to the garden and found it to be true.

In the days that followed, the beloved disciple saw Jesus and spoke and ate with him. He had seen the wonders Jesus did before his death, but God had worked no wonder like this before.

Filled with new graces by the Holy Spirit, the two disciples who discovered the empty tomb became two apostles of Christ's resurrection. Peter and John together spoke of him everywhere in Jerusalem and became pillars of his church.

Jerusalem and Samaria

Not long after the resurrection, their enthusiastic preaching about Jesus and their miraculous cure of a crippled beggar in the Temple area quickly brought them into conflict with the same Jewish leaders who had persecuted Jesus. They were called before the Sanhedrin which had assembled together to rebuke and threaten them.

"It is impossible for us not to speak about what we have seen and heard," the two apostles said in reply to their warnings.

In their early ministry in Palestine, John went with Peter to some villages in Samaria to strengthen the spirits of those who had heard about Jesus and believed in him through the preaching of the deacon Philip.

Ephesus

Then, perhaps around the year 48, tradition says John went to Ephesus in Asia Minor where for many years he guided that church by his preaching and inspired the great writings that bear his name.

Through the remaining years of his life, John's mind constantly turned to the One he began to follow at the Jordan, ever seeking to understand him and searching for words to describe him. From the ancient law he loved from his youth - Moses and the prophets - he gathered whatever he could, for Jesus had said they spoke of him.

Like an eagle, his spirits soared into the great mystery of Jesus whom he would call the Word made flesh, the Lamb of God, the Light of the world, the Bread of Life.

Yet one tradition says that as an old man this great apostle repeated one simple phrase over and over. It was a favorite saying of Jesus: "My little children, love one another."

John the son of Zebedee, the "disciple Jesus loved," lived on till an old age, some say 90 years, and was the last apostle to die.

NEW TESTAMENT WRITINGS OF JOHN

Tradition identified John the son of Zebedee with "the disciple whom Jesus loved" and the eyewitness "who testifies to these things" in the Gospel of John.

Scholars today, however, question whether John the son of Zebedee is the author of the Gospel of John according to our modern sense of authorship. So it may be better to say that the gospel preserves the memories of John the son of Zebedee while receiving its final form from one or more of his disciples.

Other writing ascribed to John, such as the letters and the Book of Revelation, may also come from the Johannine school.

WHAT LATER CHRISTIAN TRADITION SAYS ABOUT JOHN

As early as the year 135 A.D., the Christian writer Justin who visited Ephesus says that John the son of Zebedee resided in that city. Indeed, recent excavations beneath the ruins of the early church of St. John at Ephesus have uncovered a grave that may be his.

None of the apostles inspired as many stories as John did. In early Christian and medieval times, stories teaching a moral lesson from his later life and ministry abound. The following are from the Golden Legend and are immortalized in many works of medieval art.

Boiling Oil and Exile

It is said that the Emperor Domitian, hearing

that John had founded so many churches in Asia Minor, decided to kill him. So he ordered him brought as a prisoner to Rome and thrown in a vat of boiling oil that was set near the Porta Latina, a gateway to the city. The apostle was unharmed by the boiling oil, and the emperor then decided to send him into a lonely exile on the Island of Patmos. There John wrote the Book of Revelation.

When the emperor died, the Roman Senate revoked his decrees and John was free to return to Ephesus, where he was greeted by crowds of people with the same words that welcomed Jesus to Jerusalem: "Blessed is he who comes in the name of the Lord."

A Raising of the Dead

As he entered the city he met a funeral procession carrying the body of a woman named Drusiana, who had cared for the orphans and needy of Ephesus. She was John's friend and had prayed for his return. The apostle ordered them to stop and opened the top of the woman's coffin.

"Drusiana, my Master Jesus Christ raises you to life. Return to your home again," John said. And she returned to her home and prepared a feast for the apostle.

The Philosopher and the Diamonds

The next day, as John was walking in the town square, he saw a crowd listening to a famous philosopher whose name was Crato. The philosopher had just commanded two young disciples, who were very rich, to exchange everything they had for a few valuable diamonds. Then before the crowd, he had the young men smash the diamonds into small pieces to show how meaningless riches are.

Martin Schongauer. *Saint John Blessing the Poisoned Cup. With his blessing the poison departs in the form of a snake.* (15th Century)

John said to the philosopher that this was wrong. Jesus taught not to condemn riches, but to give them to the poor. "Go, sell what you have, and give to the poor," he had said to the rich young man. Gathering the fragments of the diamonds, John restored them to their original form. The two young men then followed him and gave their riches to those in need.

Rest for a Soaring Eagle

They say that when John was an old man someone gave him a beautiful bird as a gift. He loved watching the bird and holding it in his hand.

One of his followers, thinking that John was wasting his time and had better things to do, said to a companion: "Look at the old man playing with that bird like a child."

Knowing what he was thinking, John called to the young man, who always carried a bow and arrow with him.

"How do you use that bow?" John asked the young man. The youth pulled hard on the bowstring and then immediately released it.

"Why do you let go of the string so quickly?" John asked.

"Because if I held it too long, I would have no strength to launch the arrows," came the reply.

"Isn't it true also," John said, "that we cannot be doing or thinking all the time. Sometimes we need play. You know, the eagle is a bird that flies high and looks straight into the sun. But it comes back to rest on the earth. So our spirits must enjoy these little things of earth in order to search into the mysterious heavens again."

Through King Edward the Confessor, who had great devotion to St. John, devotion to the apostle called "the Divine" became a mark of the English church.

The feast day of St. John is December 27.

Mary Magdalene

"**M**ary, called Magdalene."

Women are usually described in the gospels by their husbands or children. Johanna, the wife of Herod's steward Chuza, Mary, the mother of James. For at the time of Jesus, a woman was a supporting player in a man's world; she depended on her father or husband for almost everything. Her task was to bear children and care for the home.

Mary Magdalene, however, is described by the town where she lived - Magdala - the largest town along the Lake of Galilee next to the town of Tiberias, where King Herod had his summer palace. Magdala was a thriving fishing port that sold its famous salted fish throughout Palestine and in the Greek cities beyond. Five miles north of Magdala was the town of Capernaum where much of Jesus' ministry took place.

An Unhappy Woman

Mary had no husband or children, as far as we know, so some people may have thought she had done little in life.

According to the gospels, she was a woman beset by unhappiness: she was possessed by seven devils. That seems to mean she was troubled in mind, in body and spirit.

Perhaps her health was bad, like another woman Jesus healed, whose doctors could not cure her chronic issue of blood; or perhaps she suffered in soul, like the woman whose life had been ruined by immorality. Perhaps she had mental problems.

Whatever her dark secrets, Mary was unhappy, so unhappy she could hardly go on. Indications are that she had wealth, but wealth could not remove the sorrow that followed her everywhere.

Her Healing

When Mary heard that a new prophet, Jesus of Nazareth, was healing people, she joined the crowds at the shore of the lake where he went often.

We do not know for sure how Jesus healed her, but it was probably like so many other cures the gospels record. She listened to him speak and his words themselves lifted her spirits. Afterwards she came up to him to ask for his help. He told her to have faith in God. Then he put his hands on her, and the demons were gone.

Most people healed by Jesus left quickly for home to tell their good fortune to family and friends. Mary, however, lingered on. As unhappiness left her soul and the demons were swept away, a great love awakened in her. She felt as though God had visited her through this prophet and more than anything

George Angelini. *Mary Being Healed by Jesus (Contemporary)*

else she wanted to know him. She stayed on that day and became a follower of Jesus and then his friend. She would remain till the end.

Afterwards, when Jesus went from one town and village in Galilee to another, "the twelve accompanied him," St. Luke writes, "as well as certain women who had been cured of evil spirits and sickness; Mary called the Magdalene, from whom seven demons had gone out, Johanna the wife of Herod's steward Chuza, Susanna, and several others who provided for them out of their own means."

Jesus and Women

It was unusual for a Jewish teacher to associate so closely with women. Yet Jesus did not share the prejudices against them common in his time. Women were children of God to him and not the servants of man.

He spoke out for their rights. When the Pharisees asked about the Jewish laws of divorce which notoriously favored men, Jesus took the part of the women.

"From the beginning, God made them male and female. For this reason a man shall leave his father and mother and be joined to his wife, and the two shall become one . . . What God has joined together, let no man put asunder."

Women in His Teachings

In his teachings, women often appear to have greater faith than the well-measured male responses of most Jewish leaders and even his own disciples.

Sitting in the Temple area near the treasury one day, he called attention to a poor widow who gave her two small coins as an offering, while others better off than she gave large gifts.

"She put in everything she had!" Jesus told his disciples in admiration.

At a banquet in the house of Simon the Pharisee, a woman of the town who was a sinner came and knelt before him, washing his feet with her tears, drying them with her hair, kissing and anointing them with precious oil. The Pharisee thought this out of place, but Jesus saw how right the woman's action was.

"Her many sins have been forgiven; she has shown great love," and praising the woman's faith, he told her to go in peace.

Many of his parables portray women's activities, their spirit, faith and courage. The woman searching for a lost coin, the woman measuring yeast for the mass of dough, the woman pleading with the unjust judge, portray a God who does not work only in a man's world.

Indeed Jesus respected and admired women. He was not uneasy in their presence nor did he ever patronize or slight them.

The Women Respond

Perhaps because they sensed how different he was, many women, like Mary Magdalene, approached him. And he welcomed them as if they were his own family.

"Who are my mother and my brothers?"

And looking around at those seated in the circle, he said, "Here are my mother and my brothers. For whoever does the will of God is my brother and sister and mother."

Women responded generously to him. The Samaritan woman at Jacob's well told the whole town about him. The Syro-Phoenician woman whom he met on one of his journeys was the first gentile to show faith in him. Martha and Mary, the sisters of Lazarus, opened the doors of their home to him. Mary Magdalene and some of the other women supported them from their means.

The village of Magdala was the birthplace of Mary Magdalene. The tiny village is located near the Sea of Galilee in the northern part of what was once Palestine. (Photo early 1900's.)

Women were among his most attentive listeners; they saw what he did, and they remembered everything.

Mary Magdalene: A Follower of Jesus

When Jesus went up to Jerusalem to celebrate his final Passover, Mary Magdalene accompanied, along with some other women from Galilee. Mary the mother of Jesus was among them.

That Thursday night, they heard he was arrested and in prison, and the next morning they hurried to the place where he was being held.

None of his other disciples was there; during the night they had deserted him.

Watching Helplessly

There was little the women could do except look on when Pilate pronounced the death sentence on Jesus.

All around them people shouted: "Let him be

crucified!" Nothing they could do would stop what was happening. They saw him come out bleeding from being whipped by the Roman soldiers; they watched as the wooden cross was laid on his shoulders; as he went up the path to Mount Calvary they tried to get close to him.

When he was stripped of his clothes and nailed to the cross, they could hardly bear it. But they did not leave. Instead they edged closer, until they stood near the cross itself.

Hoping Their Eyes Would Meet

Mary Magdalene stood with Jesus' mother as he hung dying on the cross. The soldiers kept them at a distance; they had no time for a victim's loved ones or their pity. His enemies continued cursing him; the cries of thieves crucified with him filled the air. But the women stayed on, unable to help. They could only stand by, hoping their eyes would meet his and Jesus would see them there.

They heard his last words:

"Father, forgive them for they know not what they are doing."

"This day you will be with me in Paradise."

"I thirst."

"Father, into your hands I commend my spirit."

Then his last cry, his bowed head and limp body told them he was dead.

The women took his body and prepared it quickly for burial, since the Passover feast had almost begun. Joseph of Arimathea offered them a tomb in a garden nearby. They buried Jesus' body at once.

Following the burial party, Mary Magdalene saw where the tomb was and planned to come back at the first opportunity to anoint the body and wrap it properly in burial clothes. Then she went back, numb with grief, to wait till the end of the feast.

"Mary!"

On Easter Sunday morning, while it was still dark, Mary came back to the tomb. The Passover had not been a time of joy for her. Instead it brought sorrow and grief to her soul.

As she approached the tomb in the dim light, she was startled to see the stone rolled away from the entrance. Believing that Jesus' body had been stolen, she ran back to tell Peter and John, "They have taken the Lord from the tomb."

Peter and John both ran to the garden with Mary following them. They went into the tomb and found only burial clothes. The two disciples went home, wondering what happened.

But Mary stayed outside the tomb weeping.

As she wept, she bent down to look within and saw two angels in white sitting there. They said to her: "Woman, why are you weeping?"

She said to them: "They have taken away my Lord, and I don't know where they laid him."

Turning around she saw Jesus there, but she did not know it was Jesus.

"Woman, why are you weeping? Whom are you looking for?" he said to her.

She thought he was the gardener and said to him: "Sir, if you carried him away, tell me where you laid him, and I will take him."

Jesus said to her, "Mary!"

She turned and said to him in Hebrew, "Rabboni!" which means "Teacher!"

Jesus said to her, "Stop holding on to me, for I have not yet ascended to the Father. But go to my brothers and tell them 'I am going to my Father and your Father, to my God and your God.' "

Saint Mary Magdalene, shown mourning at the foot of the cross, is one of the statues erected in the Convent Church in Altotting, Germany.

Mary Magdalene went to the disciples and said, "I have seen the Lord," and related what he told her.

Magdalene, Apostle to the Apostles

For the rest of her years Mary would remember those moments in the garden by the tomb. Before daybreak she had come weeping over the one she thought was lost forever. She had heard him call her name, "Mary." And she had turned to see him alive.

The dark garden turned into a paradise and she, like a new Eve, was sent by Jesus to bring news of life to all the living.

Mary was his apostle to the apostles. The belief of Christians in the resurrection of Jesus would be founded on this woman's word.

For this reason the church says to her in its liturgy every Easter Sunday:

Tell us, Mary, what did you see on the way?
"I saw the tomb of the now living Christ.
I saw the glory of Christ, now risen.
I saw angels who gave witness;
the cloths, too, which once covered head
*   and limbs.*
Christ my hope had indeed arisen.
He will go before his own into Galilee."

(Easter sequence)

What Later Tradition Says About Mary Magdalene

The New Testament says little about Mary Magdalene after the appearance of Jesus to her at the tomb. It is uncertain where she lived afterwards and where she died.

Two different traditions about Mary arose in the course of time. In the Western church since the time of Pope Gregory (7th cent.), Mary Magdalene became identified in art, liturgy and popular devotions with Mary of Bethany and the sinful woman who washed Jesus' feet (Lk 7).

According to the tradition of the Eastern church - which most modern scripture scholars follow - Mary is not the same woman as Mary the sister of Lazarus or the sinful woman of Luke's story.

In one early story from the Eastern church, Mary Magdalene accompanied Mary, the Mother of Jesus, and St. John to the city of

Caravaggio. *The Entombment of Christ* (16th Century)

Ephesus in Asia Minor and died there. Her remains were then brought to Constantinople where they were honored.

Another Eastern legend says she went to Rome to defend Christ's innocence before the emperor against Pontius Pilate and his enemies.

Mary Magdalene in the Middle Ages

According to an eleventh-century French legend, Mary Magdalene, Lazarus and Martha of Bethany, along with the two other Marys mentioned in the gospels, and St. Maximin, one of Jesus' seventy-two disciples, were sent by St. Peter to bring the Word of God to faraway peoples.

Captured by unbelievers, they were bound and thrown into a ship without a rudder and left to drown in the sea.

But God guided the ship to the port of Marseilles in France. There Mary spoke of Christ to the people.

"All were amazed," says the Golden Legend, "not only because of her beauty but also because of her eloquence. Yet how could she not be eloquent since her lips touched the Lord's feet?"

Mary brought the ruler and the people of that land to the Christian faith, according to this legend. Churches, like Les Saintes Maries de la Mer (The Holy Marys of the Sea), were built in France at an early date to commemorate the coming of these apostles from Palestine.

The Bearer of Perfume and Love

Medieval legends always picture Mary carrying a vase containing the remainder of the oil with which she anointed Jesus. And after she preached the Gospel, they say she retired to a place of prayer near the port of Marseilles called, appropriately, "La Sainte Baum," the holy anointment. There she was buried, according to this legend.

The church at Vezelay in Burgundy, claiming to have her relics, became a favorite place of pilgrimage in the eleventh century.

Mary Magdalene is a popular feminine name in France and in the rest of Europe.

Her Appeal to Christians

Mary Magdalene charmed the imagination of Christians in the Middle Ages. She appears everywhere in art, drama, poetry and spiritual writings. Medieval Christians imagined her as a beautiful, warm-hearted woman, transformed from a sinner by her love for Jesus. She was a model of what a friend and disciple of Jesus should be.

The Golden Legend, a popular collection of stories of the saints, describes her relationship to Christ this way:

(After she met Jesus) there was no grace he refused her, no sign of affection he withheld from her. He drove seven devils out of her, admitted her to his friendship, came to dwell in her house, and defended her when it was needed. He defended her before the Pharisee who accused her of being unclean, and before her sister Martha, who called her idle, and before Judas, who criticized her generosity. And Jesus could not see her in tears without weeping.

For love of her, he restored her brother to life after he had been dead for four days; he cured Martha of an issue of blood which she had suffered for seven years . . . To her the risen Jesus appeared first, and made her an apostle to the apostles.

97

Russian Church of Mary Magdalene Overlooking the Garden of Gethsemane in Jerusalem.

Imaginative Details

Fascinated by her story, medieval spiritual writers added simple human details to the gospel accounts. According to the author of the "Meditations of the Life of Christ," Mary held the feet of Jesus when he was taken down from the cross, because she had kissed them and washed them with her tears once before.

(At the tomb) she could not think, or speak, or hear anything except about him. When she cried and paid no attention to the angels, her Lord could not hold back any longer for love . . . 'Woman, whom do you seek? Why do you weep?' And she, as if drugged, not recognizing him said, 'Lord, if you carried him away, tell me where, and I will take him.'

Look at her. With tear-stained face she begs him to lead her to the One she seeks. She always hopes to hear something new of her Beloved. Then the Lord says to her, 'Mary!'

"It was as though she came back to life, and recognizing his voice, she said with indescribable joy, 'Rabbi, you are the Lord I was seeking. Why did you hide from me so long? . . . I tell you, so much grief from your passion filled my heart that I forgot everything else. I could remember nothing except your dead body and the place I buried it, and so I brought ointment this morning. But you have come back to us.'

And they stayed there lovingly with great joy and gladness. She asked him about each thing, and he answered willingly. Now, truly, the Passover feast had come. Although it seemed that the Lord held back from her, I can hardly believe that she did not touch him before he departed, kissing his feet and his hands.

Mary's Followers

Saints as well as ordinary Christians have loved this saint.

For St. Teresa of Avila (+1584), the story of Mary Magdalene played an important role in her conversion from spiritual indifference.

St. Bridget of Sweden (+1373) wrote: "There are three saints I love above all: Mary the mother of Jesus, St. John the Baptist, and Mary Magdalene."

From the Middle Ages onward, confraternities and groups under the patronage of St. Mary Magdalene worked for the reform of prostitutes and troubled women throughout Europe.

She is the patroness of perfumers, hairdressers and glove-makers.

Her feast is July 22.

Matthew, the Tax Collector

I n the days of Jesus, the town of Capernaum was blessed by nature with a beautiful lake and rich land. Living there was almost ideal, yet the Jews of Capernaum, like Jews everywhere in Palestine, had one major complaint: they had too many taxes to pay.

Almost thirty percent of what they earned went to Rome and to the rulers Rome installed in its Jewish provinces. Besides that, they owed a substantial sum to support the Temple at Jerusalem and all their religious activities. Altogether it was an intolerable burden, especially for the poor ordinary people who made up most of the population.

The Romans didn't care. They taxed their captive provinces to finance their huge military complex and to build roads, aqueducts, great marble buildings and piazzas throughout their vast empire. After counting their subjects by census, they taxed their lands, goods and whatever they sold or traded. No one escaped the net of their masterfully designed tax system.

In Palestine, the Romans left the collection of taxes to local rulers, such as Herod Antipas in Galilee. He in turn hired as tax collectors people in the local towns, instructing them how much money they were to collect. The collectors simply found out what their neighbors were worth and squeezed payment out of them to meet their quota while pocketing some of the money for themselves besides.

Feared and Despised

Certainly, some descent people entered the profession, but abuse and fraud plagued the system, so tax collectors were generally feared and despised in the towns where they lived.

Since Capernaum was along a major imperial road, it was a busy customs place where a number of tax collectors lived. Matthew was one of them.

Matthew was a Jew, the son of Alphaeus; beyond that, little of his background is known for sure.

He may have been a Levite, since he is called Levi in Mark's Gospel. Belonging to that family of Jews which traditionally took turns performing the minor tasks of doorkeepers, servers and caretakers at the Temple of Jerusalem, he may have spent a few weeks a year in Jerusalem at some work assigned to him. But since he could not live on a few weeks' salary, Matthew worked as a tax collector.

He must have been a shrewd, sharp-eyed man, able to judge goods and people quickly. A glance at someone's field or at a fisherman's

George Angelini. *Jesus and Matthew at the Tax Collector's Post (Contemporary)*

load of fish on the dock told him its worth. And he had been able to sniff out whatever contraband was hidden on a merchant's donkey travelling along the border road. That was his job, and he was probably good at it. It would make him a tidy sum.

Tight-Knit Circle of Outsiders

But being a tax collector meant one was branded and isolated in the town where one lived. People would do business with them, but otherwise Matthew and the rest of his profession met a cold politeness from their neighbors in Capernaum. They were seldom invited to homes, or meals or celebrations. Few people wanted them for friends.

So for companionship and support, the tax collectors of Capernaum and their families

101

banded together. They formed a tight-knit group and were closely connected to others in their profession throughout Palestine. Still, the stigma of being unaccepted was not an easy thing to bear.

Watching and Listening

How did Matthew meet Jesus?

As a man whose business it was to see and hear everything, he must have been aware of Jesus when the first reports spread from Peter's house and crowds began to gather. And since anyone can join a crowd, Matthew must have joined those who followed Jesus to Peter's house, to the synagogue, and to the shore of the lake.

What he saw and heard he never forgot. Certainly many of his memories of those meetings made their way into the Gospel that bears his name.

For Matthew was a profoundly religious person, a student of Jewish law. What he did as a tax collector never lessened his keen interest in the complex questions of life, which he loved to hear discussed wisely. The word of God and future of his people were dear to him.

Jesus of Nazareth was wiser than any rabbi Matthew had ever heard. He spoke simply to the crowds who came from all around to hear him, but then afterwards he would sit with a smaller group of people discussing a wide range of things contained in Jewish law: marriage and divorce, anger and reconciliation, how to deal with enemies, the limits of retaliation, prayer and almsgiving, dependence on God. The law came alive when he spoke.

Rabbis and religious experts came to dispute and question him, but they only seemed to sharpen the answers Jesus gave. These small

meetings with Jesus, which Matthew attended whenever he could, made him feel as if he were on a great mountain from which the world became even clearer and better-placed.

A Sense of Belonging . . .

Surprisingly enough, he felt welcome in these discussions. This man from Nazareth did not have the ordinary prejudices people had for tax collectors - or for anyone else for that matter. In fact, there was a goodness in him that drew Matthew and others from the town to return over and over to be at his side.

Matthew knew Jesus worked miracles. Not once but many times he saw him heal people and Matthew wondered if God's great promise of which the Prophet Isaiah spoke long ago was not being fulfilled in Capernaum of Galilee:

Galilee of the Gentiles,
the people who walk in darkness
have seen a great light,
on those dwelling in a land
overshadowed by death
light has arisen.   *(Matthew 4:14-15)*

. . . and Wonder

Was the kingdom of God coming? Was the One whom the prophets promised, the Messiah, now here? All the scripture texts Matthew knew so well he studied with a new urgency in the presence of Jesus of Nazareth.

For he saw the leper Jesus cured back again with his family; he knew the Roman centurion's servant who was painfully ill before Jesus answered his master's request to cure him; he watched a paralyzed man rise from his stretcher when Jesus spoke to him. And he heard Jesus say something that only

God should say: "Your sins are forgiven."

He witnessed so many extraordinary things and heard so much. Then, one day, Jesus called upon him.

The Invitation

He was in the customs house at the work that many thought should not be done by any good Jew. And Jesus passed by. They must have spoken for awhile, as they had spoken before, but the gospels record only the substance of their meeting that day:

"As Jesus passed by, he saw a man named Matthew sitting at the customs post. He said to him, 'Follow me.' And he got up and followed him." (Mt 9:9)

That invitation fell upon Matthew like a personal blessing. He, a tax collector, a man others avoided and called unclean, had been invited by Jesus to follow him. All the slights and insults, all the feelings of exclusion, suddenly seemed to vanish.

Tax Collector's Banquet

To celebrate their new bond, Matthew invited Jesus to a banquet at his house with his friends - other tax collectors like himself - and Jesus came with some of his disciples.

But they were criticized immediately for breaking one of Capernaum's social codes. "Why does your teacher eat with tax collectors and sinners?" some said to Jesus' disciples.

Jesus' answer was quick:

"Those who are well do not need a physician, but the sick do. Go and learn the meaning of the words 'I desire mercy, not sacrifice.' I did not come to call the righteous, but sinners" (Mt 9:12-13).

Hardly anything is known of Matthew's part in Jesus' later ministry. Certainly the tradition is correct that says he recorded much of what Jesus said and did. But are some things that happened especially related to him?

The Others Despised Outsiders

Wherever Jesus went, the gospels say, he was welcomed by tax collectors. When he entered Jericho, Zacchaeus, the chief tax

Martin Schongauer. *Saint Matthew with the Instrument of His Death* (15th Century)

collector of the city, climbed a tree to see him pass, since the crowds were so great. Did Matthew point out to Jesus the man in the tree, a tax collector like himself, and so bring them all to Zacchaeus' house, where Jesus left his blessing of salvation? And did tax collectors in other towns come to Jesus because they recognized one of their own among his companions?

Perhaps so. Like Matthew these outsiders, targets of so much suspicion, frustration and resentment, were always among those whom Jesus looked upon kindly. True, they were members of a compromising profession tainted by greed, dishonesty and bribery. Their dealings were not always according to the fine line of right or wrong. But still they were children of God, and Jesus would not let them be lost.

LATER STORIES OF MATTHEW
The Gospel of Matthew

Early Christian tradition named Matthew the tax collector the author of the first gospel. But recent studies usually describe this gospel as being written at Antioch in Syria between 80-90 A.D., so it is unlikely that Matthew was directly involved in writing the gospel as we have it. Possibly, he contributed many of the stories and sayings of Jesus found in this gospel, and through Christians at Antioch who heard him teach about his Master he became known as its author.

Certainly, the Gospel of Matthew, which tells of Wise Men coming from afar to worship the Child and tax collectors and sinners being welcomed by Christ, reflects the experience of the tax collector of Capernaum who saw himself as a stranger and outcast called by

Jesus the Messiah to be his disciple. Also, this Gospel teaches Matthew's profound respect for the law and the prophets, which are fulfilled through the coming of Christ. Reading it, we can still picture Jesus, the wise and patient Rabbi, on a mountainside near the Lake of Galilee urging his hearers to live a blessed life.

In the Gospels of Mark and Luke, Matthew is listed seventh among the apostles. In Matthew and the Acts of the Apostles, he is listed as eighth.

The Gospel of Matthew ends with Jesus, after his resurrection, standing on a mountain in Galilee, sending his disciples out to preach to all nations: "Go, and make disciples of all nations, baptizing them in the name of the Father and of the Son, and of the Holy Spirit. . . . " (Mt 28:19) Where did Matthew go after Pentecost?

There is an early tradition that says he preached in Judea to his own people; afterwards, some say, he went to Ethiopia or Persia. The various stories we have of his later ministry, however, have hardly any historical basis.

The Golden Legend, a collection of stories of saints that was immensely popular in the Middle Ages, says that Matthew went to Ethiopia where he lived in the house of the Ethiopian eunuch who was an official of the court of Queen Candace (cf. Acts 8:26ff). There he confronted two powerful magicians who used tricks to control the rulers and the people of the land. He raised the king's son to life, preached the Gospel, and converted that nation to Christianity.

Afterwards, when Matthew tried to protect a young woman from a later king's brutal

Caravaggio. *Saint Matthew and the Angel*
(16th Century)

advances, he was cut down by one of the king's soldiers as he prayed before the altar in church.

Since Matthew was a tax collector, he was honored in most large commercial cities of medieval Europe as the patron of customs officers, bankers and tax officials, who built shrines and chapels to celebrate his name. The relics of St. Matthew have been honored in the cathedral of Salerno, one of the great medieval port cities of Italy, since the early twelfth century.

The feast of St. Matthew is celebrated in the Western church on September 21, while the Eastern church honors him on November 16.

Martha, Mary & Lazarus

The Home Where Jesus Stayed

When Jesus traveled to Jerusalem he usually stayed in the little village of Bethany on the main road between the Holy City and Jericho. It was "not far from Jerusalem, just under two miles" (Jn 11:18). There, two sisters, Martha and Mary, and their brother, Lazarus, welcomed him to their home. More than a guest, Jesus was their dear friend.

The two sisters were not altogether alike. Martha, as the gospel indicates, was in charge of the house. An active woman, busy about many things and ready to speak her mind, she liked a well-run home that met everyone's needs.

And she liked doing things for others. Under her roof she wanted no one to go hungry or be without. In fact just the thought of not pleasing others completely made her anxious. The hospitable Martha cared for her household almost to a fault.

A Jewish Woman's Life

Mary shared the same tasks as her sister, for like most Jewish women then, her life followed the pattern of the busy woman praised in the Book of Proverbs:

She obtained wool and flax
and makes cloth with skillful hands.
Like merchant ships,

she secures her provisions from afar.
She rises while it is still night,
and prepares food for her household.
She picks out a field to purchase;
out of her earnings she plants a
vineyard. . .
She enjoys the success of her dealings;
at night her lamp is undimmed.
She puts her hand to the distaff,
and her fingers ply the spindle.
(Proverbs 31:13-19)

Managing their households with similar skill and dedication, Jewish women in those times kept family life among the Jews solid and strong through good times and bad.

But the Jewish woman's role was not to be just an efficient manager of her house and a caregiver for her family. She was also to be a person of sensitivity and wisdom:

She reaches out her hands to the poor,
and extends her arms to the needy. . .
She opens her mouth in wisdom,
and on her tongue is kindly counsel.
(Proverbs 31:20, 26)

Mary was such a woman of vision and wisdom. It was a dimension not shared by her sister Martha, who often seemed entangled by practical concerns. The brief story found in the gospel indicates the difference between the two women.

George Angelini. *Martha and Mary Receive Jesus into Their Home (Contemporary)*

Jesus Comes to Visit

When Jesus came once to visit, Martha immediately set about preparing an elaborate meal for him and complained when her sister Mary remained listening to Jesus' words.

"Lord, are you not concerned that my sister has left me alone to do all the serving? Tell her, please, to come and lend me a hand."

But Jesus reminded Martha that listening to what he had to say was more important than preparing an elaborate meal for him:

"Martha, Martha, you are fretting and disturbed about many details; there is need for only one thing. Mary has chosen the best; it shall not be taken from her."

The Death of Lazarus

Yet Jesus loved all three of these good people as his own family. And so when Lazarus was dying, the sisters sent word to Jesus to come.

"Lord, the one you love is ill."

107

A native boy stands with his head bowed before the traditional tomb of Lazarus, located in Bethany on the slopes of the Mount of Olives, about two miles from Jerusalem. It was here that Christ raised Lazarus from the dead.

Before he came, however, Lazarus died and was buried immediately, according to Jewish custom.

Four days after the burial, Jesus went to Bethany. Martha, hearing that he was coming, left her sister Mary mourning at home and went to meet him.

"Lord, if you had been here my brother would not have died," she said.

"Your brother will rise," Jesus said to her.

"I know he will rise, in the resurrection on the last day," Martha replied.

"I am the resurrection and the life," Jesus told her. "Whoever believes in me, even if he dies, will live, and everyone who lives and believes

in me will never die. Do you believe this?"

She said to him, "Yes, Lord, I have come to believe that you are the Messiah, the Son of God, the one who is coming into the world."

Then Martha sent for her sister Mary who came with a large group of mourners. She fell at Jesus' feet and repeated her sister's words:

"Lord, if you had been here my brother would not have died."

Deeply moved, Jesus wept.

"Where have you laid him?" he asked, and they took him to Lazarus' tomb.

The tomb was a cave, with a large stone set in its opening.

Jesus said: "Take away the stone."

"Lord, by now there will be a stench; he has been dead for four days," Martha said.

But they rolled the stone away and Jesus prayed:

"Father, I thank you for hearing me. I know you always hear me. . ."

Then he said in a loud voice: "Lazarus, come out!"

The dead man came out, tied in burial bands. So Jesus said to them: "Untie him and let him go."

It was nearly Passover when this extraordinary event took place. Before the feast they gave a dinner for Jesus. Martha served, while Lazarus was one of those who sat at the table.

During the meal, Mary took a jar of costly perfume and anointed the feet of Jesus, drying them with her hair. The whole house was filled with the fragrance.

It was the last touching tribute Jesus received from these friends who loved him beyond measure. From the house in Bethany filled with fragrance he went to Jerusalem to his death.

WHAT LATER TRADITION SAYS ABOUT MARTHA, MARY AND LAZARUS

The town of Bethany can easily be found today on the main road between Jerusalem and Jericho. Since the third century a church has marked the famous tomb of Lazarus. The story of his resurrection from the dead has been retold in the church's Lenten liturgy since the earliest centuries.

Little is known, however, about the activity of Martha, Mary and Lazarus after Jesus' resurrection, but legends - mostly unreliable - grew in time about the three.

Stories from the east place them as refugees in Cyprus, where Lazarus becomes a bishop of that region. Their relics were honored in Constantinople in the ninth century.

French Traditions About Martha

Eleventh-century French legends, however, report Lazarus becoming bishop of Marseilles in southeastern France and suffering martyrdom under the Emperor Domitian.

From these same legends came a folktale of Martha which was popular in Europe in the Middle Ages:

In the dark forest along the shores of the Rhone River, near the village of Tarascon in southern France, a great dragon lived. It killed anyone traveling on the river and sank their ships.

The people of the region called on St. Martha and she went to meet the dragon.

When it reared up to kill her she threw holy water on the monster and held up a cross before it. At once the dragon became as meek as a lamb and came quietly to her side. She put a leash around its neck, led it away, and the people put it to death with spears and stones.

Martha is still honored today in the town of Tarascon with a church in her name and a festival on her feast, July 29.

A view of the town of Bethany today.

James, the Son of Alphaeus

James, the son of Alphaeus, came from Nazareth. His mother, Mary, was related closely to Mary, the mother of Jesus. So James knew Jesus very well, for families in small towns like Nazareth were close-knit.

The Jews valued families as a way to survive and get ahead. Brothers and sisters, uncles and aunts, cousins and grandparents worked, celebrated, and often lived nearby whenever they could. They helped each other harvest foods and sew clothing: their children played together. For them, the well-being of their family was important and its good name something to be treasured.

'The Less'

James was called "the Less," perhaps because he was smaller or younger than others in his family. Yet he was no less industrious or religious than anyone else. In fact, even as a child he observed with exactness the Jewish traditions that Nazareth so tenaciously preserved.

It seems unlikely that James, along with most of his family and the people of Nazareth, noticed anything unusual about Jesus as a child or as a youth. Probably about the same age, James worked and played with him. Yet, as the gospels note, Jesus lived an unremarkable life at Nazareth; he was just the son of Joseph the carpenter, and Mary was his mother.

And so the people of Nazareth, and even his family, were taken by surprise when Jesus as a young man returned to their town after a time spent in the Jordan valley where John the Baptist was preaching and baptizing. He seemed to be transformed as he spoke eloquently in their synagogue, accompanied now by followers who called him a teacher and prophet.

The people of Nazareth, however, were not impressed: "Isn't he the carpenter's son? Where did he get such wisdom and mighty deeds?" they asked.

"A prophet is not without honor except in his native place and in his own house," Jesus replied. He left Nazareth and hardly ever returned to the place.

His family, however, would not let him go without trying to talk some sense into him. Perhaps he had gone out of his mind, or was the victim of some brief religious enthusiasm? So when they heard he had gone to Capernaum and crowds of people were excitedly following him, some of his family - James was likely among them - went there to try to persuade him to come home. They did not succeed and for a good while they were embarrassed by him.

Risen Christ Appears to Him

How did James come to believe in Jesus? We don't know. Certainly it was by the time Jesus was arrested and crucified, because James' mother Mary accompanied Mary the Mother of Jesus to Jerusalem and stood with her on Calvary. And after Jesus rose from the dead, one of the first people to whom he appeared was James.

In the years after Jesus' resurrection, James assumed a position of importance in the church of Jerusalem.

After the outpouring of the Holy Spirit at Pentecost, the twelve preached at Jerusalem, giving "testimony to the resurrection of Jesus Christ, and great grace was in them all." Pilgrims who came from all parts of the world heard their preaching, believed their word, and took their new faith back to their own cities and provinces. For the next decade, the infant church grew in the city despite occasional conflict with its ruling authorities.

Then, in the year 41, Herod Agrippa, the grandson of Herod the Great, was given authority over Judea and Jerusalem by the Emperor Claudius. The new ruler, anxious to please the Jewish ruling class, became a generous patron of the Temple and city's institutions. He also began a persecution of the Jewish Christians who had become an increasing annoyance in the city. Finally he ordered James, the son of Zebedee, killed by the sword, and this caused Christians to leave the city in great numbers.

Leads Jerusalem Church

Following the persecution, James the son of Alphaeus became more important in the church at Jerusalem as the apostles left the city one by one. He was a natural leader for the church that remained.

Spinello Aretino. *Saint James* (14th Century)

A devout Jew, James loved his ancestral Jewish piety and its rich tradition. Change and controversy were distasteful to him. He believed that his own people would come to faith in Jesus by seeing Christians living holy lives according to the law of Moses. His predominantly Jewish-Christian flock, many of them converted Pharisees, held the same opinion.

So the church under James became a church less likely to antagonize the Jewish ruling class in Jerusalem. They shared the customs and religious life of other Jews. James, in fact, was considered by all Jerusalem to be a pious and holy man.

Yet, as the Gentiles in increasing numbers embraced the Christian faith elsewhere, especially through the missionary activity of Paul, the Jewish Christians of Palestine became divided about how these new converts should live. Their judgment was important, for they were the church of the apostles. Some said the gentiles should be strictly held to follow all the Jewish practices; others, like James, saw another way.

Speaks at Jerusalem Council

The question was so important that the apostles and other leaders gathered in Jerusalem and after much debate settled the matter. Siding with Peter, Paul and Barnabas, James said:

"I hold we should not make difficulties for those Gentiles who turn to God. . ."

While he would not bind them to follow the law, the apostle urged the gentiles to respect Jewish customs followed by so many of his people, for he wanted the ancient traditions honored.

After Herod Agrippa died in 44, Rome appointed a succession of cruel and corrupt procurators who governed Palestine for the next four decades. The people grew more restless under the Roman yoke, and calls for a violent uprising increased everywhere - except among the Jewish Christians, who became more and more unpopular. Periodic famine only made matters worse.

His Death in Jerusalem

In the year 62, at a time between one procurator's death and the arrival of his successor, the high priest Hanan, summoning the Sanhedrin, brought James before it and accused him and some others of violating Jewish law. Some say he was thrown from the high tower of the Temple and beaten to death in the valley below.

Afterwards, moderate leaders among the Jews, angered by this injustice, denounced the high priest to the new procurator, who deposed him from office.

Two years later, Jewish uprisings occurred throughout Palestine as Roman tyranny increased. For six years the country was convulsed in brutal war, until in the year 70 Jerusalem fell to the Roman army, which leveled its proud buildings to the ground and killed or enslaved its entire population.

Beforehand, many of the Jewish Christians belonging to the great church of Jerusalem that James had governed left the city and fled to Pella beyond the Jordan. After the Roman wars, some of them returned and settled near their beloved city again.

New Testament Writings and James

An ancient tradition in the Western church identifies James, the son of Alphaeus

The Old City of Jerusalem, a twenty-one acre enclosure that embraces the cherished shrines of the world's three major monotheistic religions - Judaism, Christianity, and Islam. This aerial view of the Old City of Jerusalem looks east, from the Jaffa Gate and the Citadel (Herod's Palace) in the foreground to the Mount of Olives and the Garden of Gethsemane in the background, beyond the walls. The single most important Christian shrine in the Old City of Jerusalem is the Church of the Holy Sepulcher (domed structure at far left center), build in the fourth century by the Emperor Constantine on the traditional site of Jesus' crucifixion, burial, and resurrection. Just to the far left of this Church winds the Via Dolorosa, traditionally regarded as the route Jesus walked to the Crucifixion.

(mentioned among the apostles in Mt 10:3; Mk 3:18; Lk 6:15 and Acts 1:13) with James the Less (cf. Mk 15:40, Mt 27:56 and Lk 24:10).

The Eastern church sees two distinct figures: James the son of Alphaeus, an early apostle of Jesus, and James the bishop of Jerusalem, who was a relative of Jesus.

Modern scholars also differ about the matter.

The New Testament Epistle of James is

traditionally said to be the work of James, the leader of the Jerusalem church, written to Jewish Christians urging them to live moral lives as "doers of the world, not merely hearers."

WHAT LATER TRADITION SAYS ABOUT JAMES

Later stories about James like those in the Golden Legend describe him as a great ascetic who from his youth never took strong drink or meat and who wore simple clothing. He spent so much time kneeling in prayer that his knees were as much calloused as the soles of his feet.

They say too that James looked so much like Jesus that he could sometimes be mistaken for him, and for this reason many people reverenced him throughout his life. For the same reason Judas had to lead the soldiers into the Garden of Gethsamane and point Jesus out to them so that they would seize the right person.

Since the sixth century the Roman church has celebrated the feast of James along with the apostle Philip. Today the feast day is May 3.

Simon & Jude

S aints Simon and Jude are mentioned only a few times in the New Testament. They appear on lists of the apostles as tenth and eleventh respectively.

Simon is called "the Canaanite" and "the Zealot," either because he was zealous for the Jewish law or because he was a member of the Zealot party, which in the time of Jesus sought the overthrow of Roman domination by force of arms.

Some of Jesus' followers, as the gospels indicate, were far from being advocates of nonviolence. Peter was ready to use his sword in the Garden of Gethsemane when the Temple guards came to seize Jesus. And James and John told Jesus to call down fire from heaven on the hostile Samaritans whom they met on their journeys to Jerusalem.

Simon, therefore, may have had dreams of revolution on his mind when he answered Jesus' call to follow him.

Jude, called "Thaddeus" to distinguish him from Judas Iscariot, may be the brother of James, the son of Alphaeus, according to one interpretation of the gospel text. If that is so, he was also a relative of Jesus. He is often designated as the author of the Epistle of Jude in the New Testament.

Martin Schongauer. *Saint Simon, with a saw, which tradition says was the instrument of his death.* (15th Century)

115

WHAT LATER TRADITION SAYS ABOUT SIMON AND JUDE

A variety of traditions from different parts of the Christian world - all difficult to prove historically - locate the ministry of these apostles in places as far apart as Britain and Persia.

A famous legend from third-century Syria describes the mission of the apostles in the Syrian city of Edessa:

> *King Agbar of Edessa wrote a letter to Jesus in the days of his ministry in Palestine, asking him to come to the city of Edessa. For the king had heard that Jesus healed without drugs or herbs, that he made the blind see again and lepers become clean. The king himself was sick and begged the Lord to come and cure him.*
>
> *Jesus replied, praising the king for his faith, since he believed in someone he had not seen, but he regretted he could not come to Edessa since he had to finish his mission in Jerusalem. Someday, though, one of his disciples would come to heal his affliction and give life to the people of his city.*
>
> *After Pentecost, Jude was sent to Edessa and healed those who were suffering from disease. He went to King Agbar and healed him too. And the king called all his people to come and listen to the apostle, who spoke to them about Jesus who died and rose again in Jerusalem. And the king and his people believed in his words.*

According to this same tradition, Simon the

Martin Schongauer. *Saint Jude holds a club which tradition says was used to kill him.* (15th Century)

apostle joined Jude and was martyred together with him in Babylonia for preaching the Christian faith. Some Greek traditions identify Simon as the bridegroom at the marriage in Cana in Galilee.

Their feast day in the Roman calendar is October 28.

Philip & Bartholomew

Philip and Bartholomew are mentioned only a few times in the New Testament. John's Gospel recalls that Philip came from Bethsaida along the Sea of Galilee, the same town where Peter and Andrew came from. Jesus invited Philip to become his disciple near the River Jordan when John the Baptist was baptizing there.

Philip then told his friend Nathaniel, "We have found the one of whom Moses wrote in the law, and also the prophets, Jesus, the son of Joseph, from Nazareth."

Nathaniel said to him, "Can anything good come from Nazareth?"

Philip said to him, "Come and see."

Later in the ministry, Philip was present when Jesus multiplied the loaves and the fish for the crowd who accompanied them.

And shortly before Jesus' death Philip brought to Jesus some Gentiles who requested that he introduce them to his master.

Bartholomew is listed among the apostles, but nothing certain is known about him. Some think he is also Nathaniel whom Jesus saw under the fig tree and called "an Israelite without guile."

Fresco of the Martyrdom of Saint Bartholomew from the Basilica of Saint Bartholomew in Rome.

117

WHAT LATER TRADITION SAYS ABOUT PHILIP AND BARTHOLOMEW

The fourth-century Christian historian Eusebius, citing an ancient source, writes that Philip lived in Hieropolis, a city about a hundred miles inland from Ephesus, with his four daughters who were influential spiritual leaders in the church of that region. ". . .their tomb and their father's are to be seen in Hieropolis in Asia."

A later source claims that Philip was crucified for his faith on May 1. His body was afterwards brought to Rome and honored at the Basilica of the Twelve Apostles beside that of the Apostle James. Because of their common burial place the Roman Catholic church celebrates the memory of Saints Philip and James together on May 1.

Various traditions point to Ethiopia, Persia, Armenia and India as places where the apostle Bartholomew labored. Legends about Bartholomew emphasize that he cured many sick people by his healing power.

In the tenth-century, relics supposedly of the apostle were brought to Rome and placed in a church on the Tiber island where once the ancient Romans brought their sick to a healing spring dedicated to the god Aesculapius. A large hospital has stood on the site through the centuries.

The feast day of St. Bartholomew is August 24.

Spinello Arentino. *Saint Philip* (15th Century)

Thomas

Thomas, "the name means twin." In the few places of his Gospel where St. John introduces the Apostle Thomas, he does it with those words. No mention is made of Thomas' birthplace or family in the gospels. Most likely he was a Galilean who lived near the Sea of Galilee. Possibly he was also a fisherman.

As one of Jesus' twelve disciples, Thomas was an eyewitness to many of the things Christ did and he heard much of his teaching. Yet he was not an apostle who belonged to the inner circle of Jesus' companions - like Peter, James and John. If the slight indications in the gospels reveal anything about him, it is that he found Jesus hard to understand.

True, he was loyal. When the news that Lazarus was near death was brought to Jesus and the Lord told his disciples that he was going to his friend's side even though that journey was dangerous because of his enemies, Thomas said bravely: "Let us also go to die with him." (Jn 11:16)

Thomas, the Loyal Doubter

For all his loyalty to Jesus, however, Thomas did not find him easy to understand. He was not as quick or as ready to believe as the other disciples.

Yet his own groping questions often evoked some of Jesus' most memorable words.

When Jesus promised his apostles at the Last Supper that he was going to prepare a place for them and they would know the way to this heavenly kingdom, Thomas said, "Master, we do not know where you are going: how can we know the way?"

"I am the way and the truth and the life. No one comes to the Father except through me," Jesus replied (Jn 14:5).

Thomas' most significant role in the gospel story came after the resurrection of Jesus from the dead. Absent when Jesus first appeared to his disciples in the upper room, Thomas would not believe them when they said, "We have seen the Lord!"

"Unless I see the mark of the nails in his hands and put my finger into the nailmarks and put my hand into his side, I will not believe."

A week later Jesus appeared to his disciples again and this time Thomas was with them.

"Put your finger here and see my hands, and bring your hand and put it into my side, and do not be unbelieving, but believe."

Thomas answered Jesus, "My Lord and my God!"

After the coming of the Holy Spirit at Pentecost, the New Testament says nothing about Thomas or his activity.

119

George Angelini. *"Put your finger here and see my hands, and bring your hand and put it into my side, and do not be unbelieving, but believe." Thomas answered Jesus, "My Lord and my God!" John 20:27-28 (Contemporary)*

WHAT TRADITION SAYS ABOUT THOMAS

Writings attributed to Thomas the apostle appeared in the Christian churches of the East at an early date. One of them, the Gospel of Thomas, which relates details about the childhood of Jesus, was viewed as dangerous by Christian leaders of the time:

"And of the New Testament, read the four Gospels only. The others are apocryphal and harmful. The Gospel of Thomas, written by Manicheans, corrupts the souls of simple people." (St. Cyril of Jerusalem, Cat.)

The Acts of Thomas, written in Syria in the early third century, is an account of the missionary journey of Thomas to India where he dies a martyr.

All attempts to prove from this account the story of Thomas' missionary work in India as an historical fact have failed so far. True, some details of this work are accurate. Trade between Syria and India by boat and land routes was firmly established in apostolic times.

The Acts of Thomas, however, is not so much an historical document as a series of often delightful stories about the reluctant disciple's journey in a strange land. Here is how it begins:

In Jerusalem after Pentecost, the apostles, commanded by Jesus to go to all nations, met together and divided the world into sections. Then they drew lots for the place where each one was to go. Thomas drew India, and the choice did not please him at all.

"I'm a Jew," he said. "How can I go and preach to Indians?"

That night Jesus appeared to him in a dream and said: "Don't be afraid, Thomas, go to India and preach there. My grace will be with you."

But Thomas was unconvinced.

"Send me somewhere else, Lord. I'm not going to India. It's too far away."

Now the next day a certain merchant from India came to the city. His name was Abban and he had been sent by King Gundaphorus to buy a slave who could work as a carpenter for him.

Now the Lord saw Abban walking in the marketplace at noontime and said to him: "Do you want to buy a carpenter? I have a slave who is a carpenter and I want to sell him."

He pointed out Thomas who was standing nearby.

Then and there they struck a deal, and the Lord called Thomas and led him to the merchant.

"Is this your Master?" the merchant asked Thomas.

"Yes, he is my Lord," Thomas replied.

"I bought you from him," Abban said.

And the apostle said not one word.

The next morning Thomas prayed: "I will go wherever you will, Lord Jesus, your will be done." And he went off with Abban the merchant, carrying with him nothing at all.

After a long journey the two finally reached India and Abban brought Thomas to King Gundaphorus.

"What kind of work can you do?" the king asked him.

"Carpentry and building," the apostle answered.

"What can you build?"

"Ploughs and pulleys, ships and oars, houses and royal palaces."

"Can you build me a palace? " the king then asked.

"Yes I will build you a palace, for that is why I came," Thomas told him.

So the king took him outside the city gates and Thomas drew a plan for the palace on the ground and the king was most pleased with the apostle's skills. After leaving him money to begin the project, the king went away.

Now there were so many poor people in the place that instead of building the palace Thomas gave the king's money to the poor and afflicted. "The king will always have what he needs, but the poor must have something now," he said.

When the king returned to the city, his friends told him what Thomas was doing:

"He has built no palace or anything else, but goes about the city giving whatever he has to the poor. He teaches about a new God. He heals the sick and does many other wonderful things. Perhaps he is a magician?

"But he is so kind. He asks nothing for himself. He does not live extravagantly. He is someone close to God."

The king called Thomas to come immediately, and he asked him, "Have you built my palace?"

"Yes, I have built it," Thomas answered.

"When will I see it?" the king asked angrily.

"You can not see it now, but sometime later you will see it," Thomas said.

The king ordered Thomas thrown into prison and began to consider what kind of death he should suffer.

But that night the king's favorite brother Gad fell sick and died. Angels took his soul to heaven and showed him a beautiful heavenly palace, more splendid than anything he had ever seen.

"Let me dwell there," Gad said to the angels.

"You cannot dwell there," the angels answered," for that is the palace Thomas built for your brother."

"Well then, let me go back to my brother and buy it from him."

And so they permitted him to return to the earth. He told his brother what he saw and asked if he could buy his treasure.

The king replied: "I cannot sell that palace to you. I pray that someday I may live in it myself and be worthy of that place. But I can show you a man who will build you such a palace too."

So the king had Thomas released from prison and he and his brother and many of his people believed in Christ through the ministry of the apostle.

The feast day of St. Thomas is July 3.

Martin Schongauer. *Saint Thomas holding a lance which is said to be the instrument of his death* (15th Century)

Stephen, the First Martyr

Stephen, the first Christian martyr, was stoned to death in Jerusalem by an angry crowd - Paul of Tarsus was among them - about the year 35 or 36 A.D. Most likely, his death occurred during the Jewish feast of Pentecost or Tabernacles when many visitors came to the city to worship in the Temple.

Conflicts in the Early Church

By the year 35 the Christian community in Jerusalem had grown in numbers. Besides Aramaic-speaking Jews like the disciples from Galilee, some Greek-speaking Jews in the city had also become believers in Jesus.

The two groups shared a belief in Christ, but the Aramaic and Greek-speaking Christians had their differences. Their language, customs, family and regional loyalties were not the same, and as one would expect, some friction arose between them.

Greek-speaking Christians complained to the apostles that their widows and orphans were not being cared for fairly. So, to remedy the situation, the apostles appointed seven deacons to minister to their needy in the city. Stephen was the deacon to be appointed.

Stephen soon went beyond helping widows and orphans. An intelligent, skillful debater, he began zealously proclaiming the Christian message to Greek-speaking Jews coming to Jerusalem in pilgrimage. Going to the places where they met with others from their own cities and regions, he argued the Christian cause fervently and sometimes hotly. His words stirred up violent controversy in the Greek-speaking synagogues of the city.

Was Stephen a Samaritan?

Almost nothing is known about Stephen's early life or background. Some think he came from the cultured Greek city of Sebaste in Samaria, not far from Jerusalem. As someone from Samaria he was bound to cause antagonism in the Holy City.

Feuding between Jews and Samaritans was centuries old. The rivalry began even before the death of Solomon (928 B.C.) when the northern kingdom of Israel split from Judea, the kingdom of the south. Between the two regions there was continual bad feeling which erupted sometimes into open warfare.

It is hard to understand why so much bad blood existed among people who had so much in common. Their ancestors were among the tribes that escaped from Egypt and settled in Palestine. Both Jews and Samaritans honored the law of Moses and looked for a promised Messiah.

George Angelini. *The Stoning of St. Stephen (Contemporary)*

But after the Assyrians, the Greeks and Romans came to conquer the northern kingdom, great numbers of gentile colonists migrated to the Samaritan territory and mingled with the native Jews. As a result, Jews elsewhere never quite trusted the "Jewishness" of their neighbors in Samaria.

Rejecting the Temple of Jerusalem

One issue, however, was a major contention between the two peoples. The Samaritans rejected the Temple of Jerusalem as the center of Jewish worship. In Samaria they had their own Temple on Mount Gerizim.

"Our ancestors worshiped on this mountain, but you people say the place to worship is in Jerusalem," the Samaritan woman said to Jesus at the well near Sychar (Jn 4:20).

Tempers flared over the issue. Pilgrims traveling through Samaria to Jerusalem, for example, were often treated with hostility in the Samaritan towns along the way. Fighting, even incidents of killing, occurred between Jewish pilgrims and the Samaritan villagers. And so, even though the shortest route from Galilee to Jerusalem was through Samaria, Jews from that region preferred traveling the longer route through the Jordan Valley rather than through hostile Samaria.

Stephen's Discourses

Stephen's speech in the Jerusalem synagogues, as it is recorded in the Acts of the Apostles, seems to echo this old feud. Unlike the apostles, who revered the Temple and their Jewish traditions, Stephen called for a break from these sacred Jewish institutions and he upbraided his hearers:

"You stiff-necked people . . . you always oppose the Holy Spirit, just like your ancestors.

. . .They put to death those who foretold the coming of the righteous one, whose betrayers and murderers you have now become." (Acts 7:51-52)

Stoned by His Enemies

Infuriated by his attacks, Greek-speaking Jews from the Synagogue of Freedmen - traditional enemies of the Samaritans - brought Stephen before the Sanhedrin for trial.

"He never stops saying things against our holy place and the law," they charged. "For we have heard him claim that this Jesus the Nazarean will destroy this place and change the customs that Moses handed down to us." (Acts 6:13-14)

We don't know whether Stephen's death resulted from an official trial by the Jewish authorities or whether it was caused by an incensed group of his enemies taking the law into their own hands. The account in the Acts of the Apostles is unclear.

His death itself, though, is described in that account in a few powerful sentences.

As his enemies surrounded him,

Stephen, filled with the Holy Spirit, looked up intently to heaven and saw the glory of God and Jesus standing at the right hand of God, and he said, 'Behold, I see the heavens opened and the Son of Man standing at the right hand of God.'

But they cried out in a loud voice and rushed upon him together. They threw him out of the city and began to stone him. The witnesses laid down their cloaks at the feet of a young man named Saul.

As they were stoning Stephen, he called out, 'Lord Jesus, receive my spirit. Then he fell to his knees and cried out in a loud voice, "Lord, do not hold this sin against them" and when he said this, he fell asleep. (Acts 7:55-60)

125

Young Saint Stephen.

Persecution of Jerusalem Christians

Following Stephen's death, many Greek-speaking Christians fled the city, since a persecution led by zealots like Saul of Tarsus had broken out against them in Jerusalem. They scattered to Samaria and the Judean countryside where they brought their faith to the peoples of those regions. Friends took the body of Stephen and buried it.

The apostles and the Aramaic-speaking Christians living in Jerusalem were almost untouched by the persecution.

STEPHEN'S PLACE IN LATER CHRISTIAN HISTORY

St. Stephen had a special place of honor in the early church. The report of the discovery of his burial place in 415 A.D. created a sensation throughout the Christian world, which then faced a troubling future.

The barbarian invasions of Roman Europe began in the first decade of the fifth century. In the winter of 406, barbarian warriors crossed the Rhine River into Gaul, and in 409 A.D. fierce tribes of Vandals swept into much of Spain. In 410 the Visogoth leader Alaric shocked the Roman world by conquering and plundering the city of Rome itself. The Roman Empire began to fall.

Christians within the empire knew they needed a courageous faith in times like these. So they welcomed as a sign from God news from Palestine in 415 A.D. that the grave of St. Stephen had been found.

The priest Lucianus found the grave marked with Stephen's name outside the little town of Jemmala some twenty miles northwest of Jerusalem. Immediately, with great celebration, the Christian bishops and people of Palestine took Stephen's remains to Jerusalem, where a church was later built in his honor.

At that time, numbers of refugees from Spain had come to the Holy Land fleeing the barbarian invasions; among them, a priest named Orosius. He obtained some of Stephen's precious relics and returned to the western provinces where they were welcomed everywhere as visible reminders of the heroic saint's presence and power.

On his way through North Africa, Orosius presented some relics to St. Augustine, the bishop of Hippo, who saw the discovery of Stephen's remains as an example of God's care for his people. When the Vandals threatened North Africa, Augustine wrote, God chose to reveal his courageous martyr Stephen, like a treasure hidden in a field, and sent him to encourage his people in their trials.

During those turbulent days when people experienced sufferings caused by fierce barbarian raids, the figure of St. Stephen brought hope to Christians. In their suffering and exile were they not reliving his story and the story of the early Jerusalem church? The Roman Empire would fall, but the Church of Christ would remain and grow.

From that time on, Stephen's feast day has been celebrated in the Western Christian calendar on December 26, the day following the birth of the Savior. His name was also inserted then in the list of martyrs in the Roman Canon of the Mass following John the Baptist.

Paul

A few years after Jesus was born in Bethlehem, St. Paul was born as Saul in the Greek city of Tarsus in Asia Minor (now part of Turkey). As "the Apostle to the Nations," Paul would bring the message about Jesus to the world beyond Palestine.

Tarsus: "No Mean City"

He was well prepared for such a task. Tarsus was a great city of the Roman Empire, a center on the busy trade routes of Asia Minor. Like many Jewish merchant families that settled in the larger towns and cities outside of Palestine, Paul's family made a living buying and selling. They knew so much more of the wide world than the farmers of Nazareth or the fishermen of Galilee did.

From his youth Paul met merchants and travelers from many distant places: Greeks and Romans from Corinth, Thessalonica, Philippi, Ephesus, the islands of Crete and Cyprus, and even from faraway Rome.

Quick and intelligent, Paul spoke the Greek language the traders and merchants spoke. He heard about the places they came from, their customs and beliefs. He even learned in the shops of the city a trade that would support him all his life - making cloth for tents.

Yet Tarsus was more than a city of merchants and trade. It was also a center of culture and learning. Its scholars were known throughout the Roman world. "Rome is full of Tarsus and Alexandria," a Roman writer said.

Like other Jews of Tarsus who did not believe that a Jew should be isolated from the world, Paul entered into the public life and culture of his city and learned its ways. He was well-educated, for his family believed in the value of education. "We pay more attention to the education of our children than to anything else," wrote Josephus, the first century Jewish historian.

We may have an idea of what Paul looked like later on in his life, if we accept a second-century witness: "He was a small man, almost bald, with crooked legs. a strong physique, his eyes set close together and his nose somewhat hooked."

Saul, Pharisee and Roman

Though he was at home in a gentile world far from the land of his ancestors, Paul loved his Jewish traditions more than anything else. His Jewish upbringing was strict, for his family followed the traditions of the Pharisees.

When he was fifteen he went to the Temple college at Jerusalem to study under the famous Rabbi Gamaliel, whom Jews and

George Angelini. *Paul Preaching in Tarsus to a Group of Believers (Contemporary)*

Christians alike revered. The young man became a learned rabbi, fiercely loyal to Jewish teaching.

Yet he never gave up his place in the world beyond Judaism. By birth he was a Roman citizen, free to come and go in the regions then firmly controlled by Rome. And Paul was proud of that citizenship and his native city.

He described himself once: "I am a Jew, a citizen of Tarsus in Cilicia, no mean city." (Acts 22:39)

Most likely, Paul was living in Tarsus from the time when Jesus began his ministry in the year 32 until his death on Calvary and his resurrection.

Afterwards when Paul heard that disciples of 129

Jesus were proclaiming Jesus as the promised Messiah risen from the dead and that many people believed what they were saying, he became alarmed.

Hurrying back to Jerusalem, he at once joined the Jews who wanted to crush the new teaching that threatened Judaism.

Saul, the Outraged Persecutor

Paul and his companions heard Stephen, the young Greek-speaking Christian deacon, preaching about Jesus. His message inflamed them to anger and those with Paul picked up stones and began to throw them at the speaker. Paul held their cloaks and gave them his approval.

Struck by their deadly shower of stones, Stephen fell to his knees.

"Lord, do not hold them responsible for this," he cried, and slumped dead to the ground.

With Stephen's death, a large-scale persecution of Christians in Jerusalem began. Paul became an agent for the Jewish High Priest and led armed bands through the city hunting down the Greek-speaking Christians in the houses and dragging them off to prison.

Hearing that Christians were in the city of Damascus, not far from Jerusalem, Paul asked for a commission from the Jewish authorities to go there and arrest them. If Christianity were not destroyed, Paul was convinced his own beloved Jewish tradition would be seriously harmed.

Incident on Damascus Road

As Paul drew near Damascus with his companions, he was suddenly surrounded by a blazing light from heaven. He fell from his horse and heard a voice say to him, "Saul, Saul,

why do you persecute me?"

He said, "Who are you, Lord?"

"I am Jesus, whom you persecute. Get up and go into the city where you will be told what to do."

Paul got up from the ground but could not see, because he was blinded. His companions, startled by what happened, led him into Damascus. For three days he was blind and neither ate or drank.

Then the Lord appeared in a dream to a Christian named Ananias who lived in the city.

"Ananias, go to the street called Straight. and look for a man from Tarsus called Saul, for he is praying."

But Ananias was afraid: "Lord, I have heard about this man. He has persecuted those who believe in Jerusalem and has come here to arrest those who call on your name."

The Lord said to him, "Go, for this man is my chosen agent to carry my name before the nations. He will suffer much for me."

Paul, the Christian

Ananias went to the house where Paul was.

"My brother Saul," he said, giving him his hand, "the Lord has sent me - Jesus - who revealed himself to you on your way here. He wishes that you see again and be filled with the Holy Spirit."

When Ananias said this, Paul regained his sight. He recovered his strength and was baptized a Christian.

Like someone born again, Paul began to see the world as though for the first time. The dramatic experience of Jesus made him look at everything again in a new way. Jesus Christ was the Messiah sent by God and Paul had persecuted him.

Caravaggio. *The Conversion of Saint Paul* (16th Century)

The three years after his conversion Paul spent quietly outside Damascus where he grew to know Jesus more and more in prayer and reflection.

First Preaching, Then a Six-Year Retreat

In the year 37, Paul suddenly went into the city of Damascus and, going to the synagogue there, preached that Jesus was the Son of God. Fortunately, some friends warned him he was in danger and helped him escape by hiding him in a basket they lowered over the city wall by night.

From Damascus, Paul went to Jerusalem. The Christians of the city were suspicious of him at first, for they remembered Paul as a persecutor of the church years before. But Barnabas, who knew of Paul's conversion, told his story to Peter and the other apostles, and they accepted him as a believer.

Once he began to preach in Jerusalem, however, threats on his life were made again. He had to leave the city.

This time he went to Tarsus, his birthplace. For almost six years he lived there quietly while his faith in Jesus grew stronger.

Barnabas Calls Paul

During the persecution begun with Stephen's death, some Christians left Jerusalem to find safety in the city of Antioch and the island of Cyprus. Antioch, near Tarsus, was the third largest city of the Roman empire, heavily populated by Greeks from far off Macedonia.

These "gentiles" heard about Jesus with great enthusiasm and wanted to become Christians themselves. So many believed, in fact, that the apostles appointed Barnabas to go and teach these new converts. Barnabas, in turn, asked Paul to join him.

Between the years 44-47 the two disciples preached the gospel with great success to non-Jews.

It was an important new stage for the church. God was calling the nations to the gospel and Paul would be his chosen agent in bringing them the message.

Commissioned by Antioch

The leaders of the church at Antioch were praying one day when the Holy Spirit spoke to them: "Set apart Barnabas and Saul for me for the work to which I have called them."

The two disciples left the city for the first of many journeys that would engage Paul for the next seventeen years of his life.

They sailed for the nearby island of Cyprus and began preaching in the Jewish synagogues there.

As they had in Antioch, they found the gentiles accepting their words more readily than the Jews. In the island's capital of Paphos, even the Roman proconsul, Sergius Paulus, became a Christian.

Continuing on to the mainland of Asia Minor, the missionaries traveled through Pisidian Antioch, Iconium, Lystra and Derbe.

Usually they preached in the Jewish synagogues in these places, sometimes provoking strong reaction from the Jews.

In Lystra there was a paralyzed man crippled from birth and unable to walk. He listened while Paul was speaking. Paul looked at him and said in a loud voice: "Stand up on your feet!"

The man leaped up and walked about, overjoyed.

The people, mostly gentiles, who saw what

This is a panorama of Kavalla, Greece, the Ancient Neapolis, where Saint Paul first landed in Europe. He landed on his way from Sanothrace to Philippi to begin the evangelization of Europe. With him were Saint Luke, "the beloved physician," Silas, a Roman citizen, and Timothy, a Greek Jew.

Paul had done excitedly cried out: "Gods have taken human form and come down to us."

They tried to honor Paul and Barnabas with flowers and sacrifices as if they were divine, but Paul shouted: "Why are you doing this? We are human beings like you. We preach about the living God who made heaven and earth."

Many of Paul's hearers became Christians.

Some of the Jews, however, were so opposed to Paul's teaching about Jesus that they dragged him outside the city and stoned him until they thought he was dead. But Paul survived the beating and went to another city.

A Serious Disagreement

As new members flocked to embrace his teaching, Paul appointed leaders for these new Christian churches before he returned to Antioch.

"The door to faith has opened for the nations," Paul told the Christian leaders at Antioch. His success among the gentiles had further convinced him that God was calling everyone, not only the Jews, to be his children.

Others, however, disagreed with what Paul had done. They wanted the Christian church to remain Jewish and new converts to adopt Jewish ways and practices. The disagreement was so serious that Paul and Barnabas went to Jerusalem to ask the apostles to settle the matter.

133

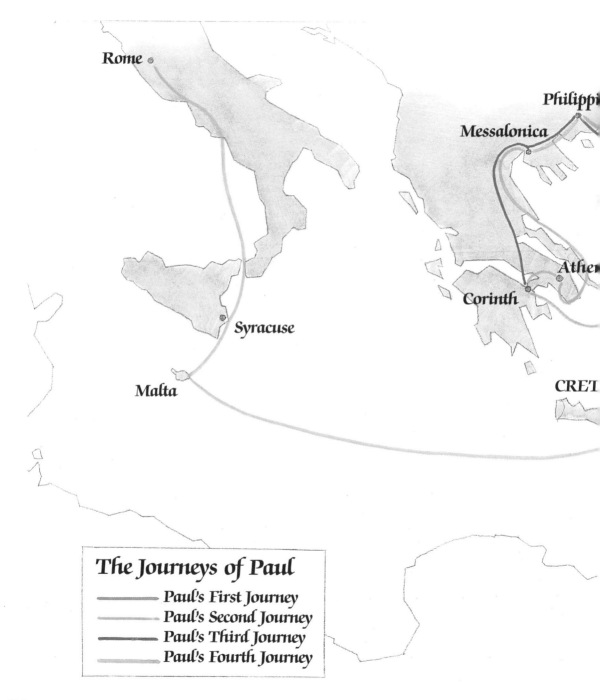

Rome

Philippi

Messalonica

Athen

Corinth

Syracuse

Malta

CRET

The Journeys of Paul

——— Paul's First Journey
——— Paul's Second Journey
——— Paul's Third Journey
——— Paul's Fourth Journey

A Major Decision

At this meeting - called the Council of Jerusalem - Peter and James approved of Paul's missionary activity among the gentiles.

Shortly afterwards, in the year 49, Paul began his second missionary journey. He revisited the Christian communities he founded, and traveled further to the more distant cities of Philippi, Corinth, Thessalonica and Athens.

In each city, people welcomed his message about Jesus. Paul cared for these new churches he founded as tenderly as a mother nursing her infants. He longed to build them up to the "Body of Christ." Like a runner in a race, he wanted to reach the whole world at once and make Christ known.

A Long and Final Third Trip

After returning to Antioch, in the year 52 Paul set out again for his longest missionary journey which ended with his death in Rome. Revisiting his many churches, he tried to be everywhere. If he could not visit in person, he sent letters to various Christian communities and individuals. His famous letters still exist: to the Corinthians, Galatians, Ephesians, Thessalonians, Romans, Colossians; to Timothy, Titus and Philemon.

Through these years. Paul met with trials as well as success. Many people loved him for his zeal; others deeply disliked him.

He listed in a letter to the Corinthians the many sufferings his missionary activity brought him:

...beatings and brushes with death. Five times at the hands of the Jews I received forty lashes less one; three times I was beaten with rods; I was stoned once, shipwrecked three times; I passed a day

and a night on the sea. I traveled continually, endangered by floods, robbers, my own people, the gentiles; imperiled in the city, in the desert, at sea; enduring labor, hardship, many sleepless nights; in hunger and thirst and frequent fastings; in cold and nakedness. Leaving other sufferings unmentioned, there is that daily tension pressing on me, my anxiety for all the churches. (2 Corintians 11:23-28)

Return to Jerusalem and Jail

In the spring of 57 Paul returned to Jerusalem. Famine had broken out in the Holy Land, and Paul had collected money from his new churches to buy food for the starving poor.

As he was going into the Temple to pray, his enemies recognized him and started a riot among the people, accusing Paul of breaking the Jewish laws of worship.

He had to be rescued by Roman soldiers guarding the city.

They took him into protective custody, and for two years he was confined in prison at Caesarea.

Unable to get a fair trial, Paul appealed as a Roman citizen to be judged by Caesar. The Roman governor, Festus, granting his request, sent him off by ship under guard for trial in Rome.

By Boat to Rome and Death

On the voyage, the ship was wrecked in a violent storm off the island of Malta. After a three-month delay on the island, the travelers finally reached Rome.

For the next two years, Paul remained under house arrest in a place he rented in the city. Free to come and go as he wished, he preached to everyone he could about Jesus Christ.

Filippo di Memmo. *Saint Paul* (14th Century)

There is a tradition that says Paul was imprisoned for a time in Rome with Peter and the two were brought to trial together and sentenced to death.

After the year 64 A.D., Paul, the great missionary, was led by soldiers outside the city in the Ostian way. They forced him to kneel on the ground and one of the soldiers beheaded him with his sword. It was a method prescribed for a Roman citizen sentenced to death.

His life's course was finished.

He had kept the faith.

The crown of eternal life that he longed for would be given to him.

Paul and the Growth of the Christian Church

About the time of Paul's death, Palestine erupted in revolt against Rome. In 66 A.D., Jewish revolutionaries seized Jerusalem from the Roman garrison and soon controlled the entire country. For almost seven years the land was torn by war and devastated until Roman legions once again ruled Palestine.

The Christian church in Jerusalem and Palestine fell rapidly into decline as large numbers of Christians fled the troubled region. Many went to Antioch in Syria, some went eastward to Mesopotamia, others to the great North African cities of Alexandria and Carthage.

Yet the new center of Christianity was to be in Asia Minor, where Paul had organized churches. In the prosperous cities and towns of that region, the new faith spread rapidly as Christian missionaries in the footsteps of Paul preached the gospel in the Jewish synagogues found throughout the area.

In a letter to the Emperor Trajan written about 112, Pliny, the Roman governor of Blythinia in Asia Minor, noted the remarkable growth of the new religion: "this contagious superstition" (Christianity) had spread through his provinces leaving the ancient temples almost empty. Asia Minor was now Christianity's most powerful base.

And Paul was its guiding leader. His letters were read over and over by his followers along with the gospels that told the stories of Jesus. Paul's spirit inspired not only the churches of Asia Minor but other churches as well. From its busy port cities and over the land routes that extended in every direction from that region, Christianity was carried to other towns and places throughout the world.

Because of the influence of his great epistles and the multitude of churches that trace their origin to his preaching, Paul is called the Apostle of the Nations.

The Feast of the Conversion of St. Paul is celebrated on January 25. The Feast of Saints Peter and Paul is celebrated on June 29.

Ann

The story of Ann and Joachim first appears in the apocryphal Gospel of James, written in the latter part of the second century. The parents of Mary, the mother of Jesus, are not mentioned in the New Testament. What follows is an adaptation of the second-century story.

The Story

Ann, the mother of Mary, was born in Bethlehem, where, years later, Jesus would be born. She married Joachim from Nazareth in Galilee. Their marriage was blessed in many ways. They loved each other very much and over the years their love only grew stronger. The couple prospered when they moved to Jerusalem where Joachim, who owned large herds of sheep, began to supply the Temple with sheep from his flocks for sacrifice.

Unfortunately, after twenty years of marriage they had no children. They prayed and prayed, and even vowed to dedicate to God any children they had. Year after year they entered the Temple to call upon God for help. But no child came.

Once, when Joachim went into the Temple for the feast of the Dedication, he overheard someone ridiculing him for not being able to father a child. Stung by the remark, he went out into the hill country near Jerusalem where the shepherds tended his flocks and cried to God about his disappointment of so many years.

The Angel's Message

After Joachim had spent many days alone there, an angel appeared to him in a dazzling light. He was frightened by the vision, but the angel said:

"Don't be afraid. I have come to tell you the Lord has heard your prayers. He knows how good you are and your sorrows for having no child.

"God will give your wife a child just as he did Sara, the wife of Abraham, and Anna, the mother of Samuel.

"Ann will bear you a daughter. You shall call her Mary and dedicate her to God, for she will be filled with the Holy Spirit from her mother's womb.

"I will give you a sign," the angel continued. "Go back to Jerusalem. You will meet your wife at the Golden Gate, and your sorrow will be turned to joy."

Meanwhile, Ann, not knowing where her husband had gone, grew anxious and afraid. She, too, was hurt that she had no children and felt as though she were being punished by God.

Going into the garden, she noticed sparrows building a nest in a laurel tree, and she began to cry:

Why was I born, O Lord?
The birds build nests for their young
yet I have no child of my own.

139

George Angelini. *Ann and Joachim with Mary (Contemporary)*

*The animals of the earth, the fish of the sea
are fruitful, yet I have nothing.
The land produces fruit in due season,
but I have no infant to hold in my arms.*

Suddenly, the angel of the Lord came to her and said, "Ann, the Lord has heard your prayer. You shall conceive a child whom the whole world will praise. Go to the Golden Gate in Jerusalem and meet your husband there."

She went quickly to Jerusalem. The two met at the beautiful Golden Gate, embraced each other and joyfully shared the angel's promise.

Returning home, Ann conceived and bore a daughter, and called her Mary.

Dedicating Mary

When Mary was three years old, her parents presented her in the Temple in Jerusalem as a gift to the Lord.

The little girl ascended the fifteen great steps to the Temple courtyard and approached the altar of sacrifice. She seemed to know already that her life was to serve God. The Temple of God was a place she loved and there was nowhere else she would rather be. God was there.

When Mary was fourteen, the time young girls then married, she wondered what her future would be. Her parents knew their child had a special place in God's plan, but what it was they did not know. They began to arrange

The Golden Gate in Jerusalem where Ann met Joachim and joyfully shared the angel's promise.

for her marriage, as was customary in those days, and sought advice from the Jewish high priest himself.

After praying for guidance, the high priest called every unmarried man from the tribe of David to come to the Temple with a branch from the fields and lay it on the altar. The one whose branch flowered, he decided, would marry Mary.

Joseph was among those who came at the high priest's call, but he brought no branch with him. Yet God pointed him out as the one who should be Mary's husband.

When Joseph finally placed a branch on the altar, it immediately flowered. The two were betrothed in marriage, and Mary returned to her parents' home at Nazareth to wait some months and to prepare for the wedding.

While she was there, the angel Gabriel appeared to her and announced that she was to be the Mother of Jesus. By the power of the Holy Spirit she conceived the Child.

After Jesus was born, Mary and Joseph returned to Nazareth where they would live for Jesus' early years. Ann and Joachim often visited them there and helped to care for the child.

From them, Jesus learned what every infant and child learned from grandparents who fondly watch their grandchildren grow and love them with all their heart.

When they died, or where, we do not know, but tradition says Jesus was with Ann and Joachim when they passed on to God.

The Story of St. Ann in Christian Tradition

This story, as we have already stated in discussing the stories of Mary, goes beyond and contrary to what the scriptures seem to indicate about Mary's early life. But it was widely circulated and had great influence in Christian art, liturgy and devotion.

No doubt the story was meant to support the traditional belief in Christ as Son of God and Son of the Virgin Mary which, at the time of the story's origin, was being attacked by heretical groups to the Christian faith.

But perhaps there is another reason for the story. Could it be that many ordinary Christians, mothers and fathers, wives and husbands, grandfathers and grandmothers, were looking for examples to follow in their own family life, and found them in Ann and Joachim?

Early Churches and Feasts

Around the year 550, a church in honor of St. Ann was built in Jerusalem on the site where she is said to have lived.

Feasts honoring Mary's birth (Sept. 8) and her Presentation at the Temple (Nov. 21) - inspired by this story - were introduced into the liturgies of the Eastern church in the sixth century. Feasts in honor of Saints Joachim and Ann (Sept. 9), the conception of St. Ann (Dec. 9), and St. Ann alone (July 25) have been celebrated from the seventh century in the Greek and Russian churches.

In the Western church, the feast of St. Ann has been celebrated on July 26 since the sixteenth century.

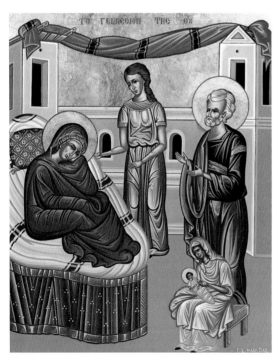

The Icon of the Nativity of the Mother of God: Saint Ann reclining on a bed with an attendant at her side. The Virgin is in the arms of a midwife who is seated on a stool. Saint Joachim is speaking with his wife.

Devotion to St. Ann in Europe

Devotion to St. Ann grew in the Western churches through popular belief that her relics had been brought to the coast of France by Mary Magdalene, Lazarus, Martha and other friends of Jesus who, it was believed, crossed the stormy sea from Palestine to bring the Christian faith to the region of Marseilles.

Her body, according to legend, was buried in a cave under the church of St. Mary in Apt by St. Auspice, the bishop. When the barbarians invaded that area, the cave was filled with debris, almost forgotten until it was dug out six hundred years later during the reign of Charlemagne.

Sailors and miners, as you see from the details of the legend, would always be devoted to St. Ann.

When the crusaders from Europe - many of them from France - went to the Holy Land in the eleventh century, they rebuilt the early church of St. Ann in Jerusalem. By the fouteenth century, devotion to St. Ann was extremely popular throughout Europe.

The Black Death: a Blow to Family Life

Devotion to St. Ann grew rapidly in Europe from the fourteenth to the sixteenth centuries. Why?

During those centuries Europe was struck by the Black Death, a plague that raged for over 150 years, wiping out twenty-five to thirty percent of the people of Europe. Fear, famine and death touched every home.

The family unit had to support the weary.

Saint Ann, Mary, and the Infant Jesus (15th Century)

Families under pressure needed models like the Holy Family - Mary and Joseph - who cared for their child in difficult circumstances.

The times called, too, for strong extended families where grandparents and other relatives would lend a hand. Ann and Joachim, who supported their offspring at Nazareth, were figures the Christians' imagination would naturally remember.

Families Under Pressure

Families came under new pressure when the plague ended and the population of Europe expanded dramatically in the late fifteenth and sixteenth centuries.

As new towns and cities sprang up everywhere, people began moving from rural areas to new places, often feeling uprooted as they left family and friends at a distance.

Work was not easy to find, and skyrocketing inflation made it hard to buy shelter, clothing or enough food.

Families could only survive through love, faith and sacrifice. Again, the biblical models of Mary, Joseph, Ann and Joachim were suggested by Christian faith.

Confraternities of St. Ann sprang up everywhere at this time - groups of Christians inspired by the kindly mother of Mary and dedicated to supporting family life by caring for widows, orphans and families under stress.

Arranged Marriages, Childlessness and Child Neglect

Little is known about family life in these difficult centuries, but we can see some of its problems. Arranged marriages were the norm, as they were in biblical time, but they seemed based more on economic advantage than personal compatibility. Young girls - and to a lesser extent young men - married at age fourteen, and sometimes feared married life rather than welcomed it. Childlessness was not unusual in these circumstances, and people commonly interpreted it as a punishment from God.

Many women, on the other hand, overburdened by too many children, gave in to depression. Neglected infants, often refused the vital nourishment of their mother's milk, were not unknown.

The examples of the nursing Madonna and

the caring grandmother Ann were important in a world trying to survive.

Saints Who Care for Children

Early child care was not well understood in the centuries when the Black Plague struck. Sickness and unending work often left children deprived of attention, affection and play they needed to develop well. The young had little schooling beyond what their families could provide.

The many images we have from this time of Mary and Ann playing with the Christ Child or John the Baptist were created for more than pious purposes. They taught lessons of bonding and child care as well.

St. Ann the Teacher

The catastrophic period of the Black Death was followed by a period of great development in Europe. The population increased rapidly and Europe became a land of cities and towns instead of farmlands. An expanding economy needed an educated and literate people.

A picture of St. Ann, popular at this time, may indicate the way devotion often responds to a need: St. Ann teaching Mary as a little child how to read.

In an age when literacy was becoming a key to the future, perhaps the saintly grandmother was showing parents what they should do that their children might have a better life. Holiness was as simple as teaching your child to read.

Shrines to St. Ann

Numerous churches and shrines to St. Ann can be found throughout Europe, the Americas, and other parts of the world. The ancient shrines of St. Ann in Jerusalem and in Apt, France, still exist. She is the patroness of French Brittany, and the great shrine of Sainte Anne d'Auray, founded in the seventeenth century, is one of the largest pilgrimage centers of Europe, especially popular with the Bretons of France.

Settlers from this region brought their devotion to Canada where they established the shrine of Sainte Anne de Beaupre near Quebec in 1638. Vast crowds visit this shrine yearly.

In the U.S., the shrine of St. Ann in Scranton, Pennsylvania, draws large numbers of people who come to honor this saintly woman who still proclaims the simple values of family life.

Church of Saint Ann, Jerusalem. (Picture in the 1900's)

Acknowledgments

The Regina Press would like to thank all those who were involved with this project, especially our dear friend Father Victor Hoagland, C.P.

George Angelini
The Byzantine Diocese of Passaic, N.J.
Art Resource, N.Y.
Catholic Art Education, Blauvelt, N.Y.
Father Flavian Dougherty, C.P.
Father Francis Finnegan
Reverend Victor Hoagland, C.P.
Reverend Sebastian Kolinovsky, C.P.
The Metropolitan Museum of Art, N.Y.
Father David Monaco, C.P.
Carol Myers
The National Gallery of Art, Washington, D.C.
Norton-Simon, California
Passionist Archives
Religious News Service
Father John Render, C.P.
Wallraf-Richartz-Museum, Cologne

Credits

68 Passionist Archives

71 Passionist Archives

74 Father David Monaco, C.P.

77 George Angelini

78 The Metropolitan Museum of Art, N.Y. Gift of George Blumenthal, 1941 (41.100.22)

79 Passionist Archives

81 Religious News Service Photo (Reproduction rights not transferable) (NR-A21)

81 Passionist Archives

82 Passionist Archives

84 Passionist Archives

87 George Angelini

89 Religious News Service Photo (Reproduction rights not transferable) (JW-BIRM-3A-8-JOG-W-C)

91 Religious News Service Photo (Reproduction rights not transferable) (P-HESS-2C-8-JOG-C)

92 Bildarchiv Foto Marburg/Art Resource,N.Y.

94 Religious News Service Photo (Reproduction rights not transferable) (WW-2)

97 George Angelini

99 Passionist Archives

101 Alinari/Art Resource, N.Y.

103 George Angelini

104 Religious News Service Photo (Reproduction rights not transferable) (FJO-NY-3B-50-JOG-PI)

105 Father David Monaco, C.P.

107 The Metropolitan Museum of Art, N.Y. Robert Lehman Collection, 1975 (1975.1.64)

109 Religious News Service Photo (Reproduction rights not transferable) (C-NY-1A-74-DS)

111 Passionist Archives

112 Passionist Archives

113 Father Victor Hoagland, C.P.

114 The Metropolitan Museum of Art, N.Y. Robert Lehman Collection, 1975 (1975.1.63)

116 George Angelini

118 Passionist Archives

120 George Angelini

122 Passionist Archives

125 George Angelini

127 Scala/Art Resource, N.Y.

129 Religious News Service Photo (Reproduction rights not transferable) (COR-ATH-5C-51-TFD-PID)

130 George Angelini

131 George Angelini

133 The Metropolitan Museum of Art, N.Y. Gift of Coudert Brothers, 1888 (88.3.99)

136 George Angelini

137 Alinari/Art Resource, N.Y.

138 The Byzantine Diocese of Passaic, NJ

139 Passionist Archives.

140 Alinari/Art Resource, N.Y.